MEXICO CITY
RESTAURANT
GUIDE 2018

RESTAURANTS, BARS & CAFES

★★★★★

The Most Positively Reviewed and Recommended Restaurants in the City

EGP
National

MEXICO CITY RESTAURANT GUIDE 2018
Best Rated Restaurants in Mexico City

© Ramon K. Gooden, 2018
© E.G.P. Editorial, 2018

Printed in USA.

ISBN-13: 978-1545123225
ISBN-10: 1545123225

MEXICO CITY RESTAURANTS 2018

The Most Recommended Restaurants in Mexico City

This directory is dedicated to the Business Owners and Managers who provide the experience that the locals and tourists enjoy. Thanks you very much for all that you do and thank for being the "People Choice".

Thanks to everyone that posts their reviews online and the amazing reviews sites that make our life easier.

The places listed in this book are the most positively reviewed and recommended by locals and travelers from around the world.

Thank you for your time and enjoy the directory that is designed with locals and tourist in mind!

TOP 500
RESTAURANTS
Ranked from #1 to #500

#1
El Cardenal
Cuisines: Mexican
Average price: Expensive
Area: Centro Sur
Address: Palma 23
06000 México, D.F. Mexico
Phone: 55 5521 8815

#2
Contramar
Cuisines: Seafood
Average price: Expensive
Area: Condesa
Address: Calle de Durango 200
06700 México, D.F. Mexico
Phone: 55 5514 9217

#3
Yuban
Cuisines: Oaxacan, Cocktail Bar
Average price: Expensive
Area: Roma Norte
Address: Colima 268
06700 México, D.F. Mexico
Phone: 55 6387 0358

#4
Pinche Gringo BBQ
Cuisines: American, Barbeque, Cafeteria
Average price: Modest
Area: Narvarte
Address: Cumbres de Maltrata 360
03020 México, D.F. Mexico
Phone: 55 6389 1129

#5
Pujol
Cuisines: Mexican
Average price: Exclusive
Area: Polanco
Address: Francisco Petrarca 254
11570 México, D.F. Mexico
Phone: 55 5545 4111

#6
Merotoro
Cuisines: Northern Mexican
Average price: Expensive
Area: Condesa
Address: Av. Ámsterdam 204
06140 México, D.F. Mexico
Phone: 55 5564 7799

#7
La Docena
Cuisines: Seafood
Average price: Expensive
Area: Roma Norte
Address: Av. Álvaro Obregón 31
06700 México, D.F. Mexico
Phone: 55 5208 0748

#8
El Cardenal
Cuisines: Mexican, Bar
Average price: Modest
Area: Centro Poniente
Address: Av. Juárez 70
06050 México, D.F. Mexico
Phone: 55 5518 6632

#9
El Balcón del Zócalo
Cuisines: Mexican
Average price: Expensive
Area: Centro Sur
Address: Av. 5 de Mayo 61
06000 México, D.F. Mexico
Phone: 55 5130 5130

#10
Cirene
Cuisines: Seafood, Bar, Tacos
Average price: Modest
Area: Roma Norte
Address: Orizaba, 87
06700 México, D.F. Mexico
Phone: 55 6840 3074

#11
Limosneros
Cuisines: Mexican
Average price: Expensive
Area: Centro Norte
Address: Av. Ignacio Allende 3
06010 México, D.F. Mexico
Phone: 55 5521 5576

#12
Cafebrería El Péndulo
Cuisines: BookStore
Average price: Modest
Area: Juárez
Address: Hamburgo 126
06600 México, D.F. Mexico
Phone: 55 5208 2327

#13
Quintonil
Cuisines: Mexican
Average price: Exclusive
Area: Polanco
Address: Newton 55
11550 México, D.F. Mexico
Phone: 55 5280 1660

#14
Qué Sería de Mí
Cuisines: Breakfast & Brunch,
Sandwiches, French
Average price: Modest
Area: Condesa
Address: Alfonso Reyes 164
06170 México, D.F. Mexico
Phone: 55 6267 6844

#15
Azul
Cuisines: Mexican, Bar
Average price: Expensive
Area: Centro Sur
Address: Isabel La Católica 30
06000 México, D.F. Mexico
Phone: 55 5510 1316

#16
Lonchería Bravo
Cuisines: Mexican, Sandwiches,
Breakfast & Brunch
Average price: Modest
Area: Cuauhtémoc
Address: Calle Río Sena 87
06500 México, D.F. Mexico
Phone: 55 5207 6276

#17
El Bajío
Cuisines: Mexican
Average price: Modest
Area: Polanco
Address: Alejandro Dumas 7
11550 México, D.F. Mexico
Phone: 55 5281 8245

#18
Gotan
Cuisines: Argentine, Barbeque, Italian
Average price: Expensive
Area: Tabacalera
Address: Pedro Baranda 17
06030 México, D.F. Mexico
Phone: 55 5535 2136

#19
Porchetta Pork House
Cuisines: Gastropubs, Steakhouse
Average price: Modest
Area: Polanco
Address: Campos Elíseos 247
11550 México, D.F. Mexico
Phone: 55 6840 0588

#20
La Capital
Cuisines: Mexican
Average price: Expensive
Area: Condesa
Address: Av. Nuevo León 137
06140 México, D.F. Mexico
Phone: 55 5256 5159

#21
Nagaoka
Cuisines: Japanese, Sushi Bar
Average price: Expensive
Area: Nápoles
Address: Arkansas 38

03810 México, D.F. Mexico
Phone: 55 5543 9530

#22
Gotan
Cuisines: Argentine, Italian, Steakhouse
Average price: Modest
Area: Centro Poniente
Address: Revillagigedo 18
06000 México, D.F. Mexico
Phone: 55 5512 6203

#23
Fonda Margarita
Cuisines: Diner, Mexican
Average price: Inexpensive
Area: Del Valle
Address: Adolfo Prieto 1364
03200 México, D.F. Mexico
Phone: 55 5559 6358

#24
Azul
Cuisines: Mexican
Average price: Expensive
Area: Condesa
Address: Calle Nuevo León 68
06140 México, D.F. Mexico
Phone: 55 5286 6380

#25
Café de Tacuba
Cuisines: Mexican
Average price: Expensive
Area: Centro Norte
Address: Calle de Tacuba 28
06010 México, D.F. Mexico
Phone: 55 5521 2048

#26
Panadería Rosetta
Cuisines: Bakeries, Cafeteria
Average price: Modest
Area: Juárez
Address: Havre 73
06600 México, D.F. Mexico
Phone: 55 5207 7065

#27
El Pan Comido
Cuisines: Vegetarian, Vegan
Average price: Modest
Area: Roma Norte
Address: Tonalá S/N
06700 México, D.F. Mexico
Phone: 55 4398 4366

#28
Hostería La Bota
Cuisines: Bar, Spanish, Mediterranean
Average price: Modest
Area: Centro Sur
Address: Peatonal San Jerónimo 40
06050 México, D.F. Mexico
Phone: 55 5709 9016

#29
El Pescadito
Cuisines: Seafood, Fast Food, Northern Mexican
Average price: Inexpensive
Area: Condesa
Address: Calle Atlixco 38
06700 México, D.F. Mexico
Phone: 55 6268 3045

#30
El Estanquillo
Cuisines: Steakhouse
Average price: Modest
Area: Condesa
Address: Acapulco 51
06700 México, D.F. Mexico
Phone: 55 5211 7632

#31
Tacos El Caminero
Cuisines: Mexican
Average price: Inexpensive
Area: Cuauhtémoc
Address: Río Lerma 138
06500 México, D.F. Mexico
Phone: 55 5514 5615

#33
Semilla Capital
Cuisines: Street Vendor, Fast Food, Hot Dogs
Average price: Inexpensive
Area: Centro Sur
Address: Plaza de la Constitución S/N
México, D.F. Mexico
Phone: 55 5106 5983

#32
Café El Popular
Cuisines: Cafeteria
Average price: Inexpensive
Area: Centro Sur
Address: 5 de Mayo 52
06000 México, D.F. Mexico
Phone: 55 5518 6081

#34
Coox Hanal
Cuisines: Yucatan
Average price: Modest
Area: Centro Sur
Address: Isabel la Católica 83
06000 México, D.F. Mexico
Phone: 55 5709 3613

#35
El Vilsito
Cuisines: Tacos
Average price: Modest
Area: Narvarte
Address: Av. Universidad 248
03020 México, D.F. Mexico
Phone: 55 5682 7213

#36
Al Andalus
Cuisines: Arabian
Average price: Modest
Area: Centro Sur
Address: Mesones 171
06000 México, D.F. Mexico
Phone: 55 5522 2528

#37
El Parnita
Cuisines: Mexican
Average price: Modest
Area: Roma Norte
Address: Yucatán 84, Roma Norte
06700 México, D.F. Mexico
Phone: 55 5264 7551

#38
Por Siempre
Cuisines: Tacos, Street Vendor, Vegan
Average price: Inexpensive
Area: Roma Norte
Address: Chiapas S/N
06760 México, D.F. Mexico
Phone: 55 3923 7976

#39
Rokai
Cuisines: Japanese
Average price: Expensive
Area: Cuauhtémoc
Address: Río Ebro 87
06500 México, D.F. Mexico
Phone: 55 5207 7543

#40
Máximo Bistrot Local
Cuisines: Modern European,
French, Mexican
Average price: Expensive
Area: Roma Norte
Address: Tonalá 133
06700 México, D.F. Mexico
Phone: 55 5264 4291

#41
Rosetta
Cuisines: Italian
Average price: Exclusive
Area: Roma Norte
Address: Colima 166
06700 México, D.F. Mexico
Phone: 55 5533 7804

#42
El Mayor
Cuisines: Mexican, Cocktail Bar
Average price: Modest
Area: Centro Norte
Address: República de Argentina 17
06020 México, D.F. Mexico
Phone: 55 5704 7580

#43
Nudo Negro
Cuisines: Mexican, Cocktail Bar
Average price: Expensive
Area: Roma Norte
Address: Zacatecas 139
06700 México, D.F. Mexico
Phone: 55 5564 5281

#44
Pan Comido
Cuisines: Delis, Vegan, Vegetarian
Average price: Modest
Area: Anzures
Address: Leibnitz 117 -3
11590 México, D.F. Mexico
Phone: 55 6386 0192

#45
El Tizoncito
Cuisines: Tacos
Average price: Modest
Area: Condesa
Address: Campeche 362 - A
06100 México, D.F. Mexico
Phone: 55 5211 5139

#46
Cantina Riviera
Cuisines: Dive Bar, Yucatan
Average price: Modest
Area: Roma Norte
Address: Chiapas 174
06700 México, D.F. Mexico
Phone: 55 5264 1552

#47
Fonda 99.99
Cuisines: Yucatan, Soup
Average price: Modest
Area: Del Valle
Address: Moras 347
03100 México, D.F. Mexico
Phone: 55 5559 8732

#48
Kolobok
Cuisines: Russian
Average price: Modest
Area: Santa María la Ribera
Address: Salvador Díaz Mirón 87
06400 México, D.F. Mexico
Phone: 55 5541 7085

#49
La Re Pizza
Cuisines: Pizza, Argentine, Italian
Average price: Inexpensive
Area: Nápoles
Address: Pensylvania 55
03810 México, D.F. Mexico
Phone: 55 5523 8683

#50
El Pialadero de Guadalajara
Cuisines: Jaliscan
Average price: Modest
Area: Juárez
Address: Hamburgo 332
06600 México, D.F. Mexico
Phone: 55 5211 7708

#51
Lalo!
Cuisines: Breakfast & Brunch,
Cafeteria, Pizza
Average price: Modest
Area: Roma Norte
Address: Calle Zacatecas 173
06700 México, D.F. Mexico
Phone: 55 5564 3388

#52
Jucy Lucy
Cuisines: Burgers
Average price: Modest
Area: Roma Norte
Address: Tabasco 46
06700 México, D.F. Mexico
Phone: 55 5207 3351

#53
Mog
Cuisines: Vietnamese, Japanese, Thai
Average price: Modest
Area: Roma Norte
Address: Frontera 168
06700 México, D.F. Mexico
Phone: 55 5264 1629

#54
Ojo de Agua
Cuisines: Mexican, Sandwiches
Average price: Modest
Area: Condesa
Address: Citlaltépetl 23c
06100 México, D.F. Mexico
Phone: 55 6395 8000

#55
La Casa de las Sirenas
Cuisines: Mexican, Bar
Average price: Expensive
Area: Centro Norte
Address: Republica de Guatemala 32
06000 México, D.F. Mexico
Phone: 55 5704 3273

#56
Anatol
Cuisines: Cefe
Average price: Exclusive
Area: Polanco
Address: Presidente Masaryk 390
11560 México, D.F. Mexico
Phone: 55 3300 3950

#57
Los Amantes Café Bistrot
Cuisines: Breakfast & Brunch, Cafeteria
Average price: Modest
Area: Condesa
Address: Sinaloa 213
06700 México, D.F. Mexico
Phone: 55 6823 0012

#58
Tortería El Cuadrilátero
Cuisines: Mexican, Delis
Average price: Inexpensive
Area: Centro Poniente
Address: Luis Moya 73
06050 México, D.F. Mexico
Phone: 55 6095 4756

#59
Yamasan Ramen House
Cuisines: Ramen
Average price: Modest
Area: Condesa
Address: Tamaulipas 103
06140 México, D.F. Mexico
Phone: 55 5211 7847

#60
123 Comida Tienda
Cuisines: Asian Fusion, Thai
Average price: Modest
Area: Centro Poniente
Address: Calle Artículo 123 123
06050 México, D.F. Mexico
Phone: 55 5512 1772

#61
Salón Tenampa
Cuisines: Dive Bar, Mexican
Average price: Modest
Area: Centro Norte
Address: Plaza Garibaldi 12
06010 México, D.F. Mexico
Phone: 55 5526 6176

#62
Mostaza
Cuisines: Bakeries, Sandwiches
Average price: Modest
Area: Polanco
Address: Emerson 243
11560 México, D.F. Mexico
Phone: 55 5171 7007

#63
Sanborns de los Azulejos
Cuisines: Cafeteria, Mexican, Local Flavor
Average price: Modest
Area: Centro Sur
Address: Av. Francisco I. Madero 4
06500 México, D.F. Mexico
Phone: 55 5512 1331

#64
Belmondo
Cuisines: Delicatessen, Sandwiches
Average price: Modest
Area: Roma Norte
Address: Tabasco 109
06700 México, D.F. Mexico
Phone: 55 6273 2079

#65
Butcher & Sons
Cuisines: Burgers, American, Gastropubs
Average price: Modest
Area: Polanco
Address: Virgilio 8
11560 México, D.F. Mexico
Phone: 55 5280 4247

#66
Restaurante El Cardenal
Cuisines: Mexican
Average price: Modest
Area: Tecamachalco
Address: Paseo de las Palmas 215
11000 México, D.F. Mexico
Phone: 55 2623 0402

#67
La Santa Gula
Cuisines: Mediterranean
Average price: Modest
Area: Coyoacán
Address: Xicoténcatl
16038 México, D.F. Mexico
Phone: 55 5914 7001

#68
Chilakillers
Cuisines: Mexican
Average price: Inexpensive
Area: Tacubaya
Address: Av. Revolución 23
11870 México, D.F. Mexico
Phone: 55 5264 2818

#69
Bellaria
Cuisines: Italian
Average price: Expensive
Area: Polanco
Address: Presidente Masaryk, 514
11560 México, D.F. Mexico
Phone: 55 5282 0413

#70
La Pagoda
Cuisines: Mexican, Cafeteria
Average price: Modest
Area: Centro Sur
Address: Av. 5 de Mayo 10
06000 México, D.F. Mexico
Phone: 55 5510 9176

#71
Recomienda
Cuisines: Mexican
Average price: Inexpensive
Area: Roma Norte
Address: Chiapas 126
06700 México, D.F. Mexico
Phone: 52 557 44437

#72
Butcher & Sons
Cuisines: Burgers, American
Average price: Expensive
Area: Roma Norte
Address: Colima 87
06700 México, D.F. Mexico
Phone: 55 5207 8121

#73
Brit Majal
Cuisines: Indian, British
Average price: Modest
Area: Condesa
Address: Puebla 242
06700 México, D.F. Mexico
Phone: 55 5208 3703

#74
Gatorta
Cuisines: Mexican, Vegan
Average price: Inexpensive
Area: Roma Norte
Address: Puebla 182
06700 México, D.F. Mexico
Phone: 55 3038 4404

#75
Primos
Cuisines: Cefe
Average price: Expensive
Area: Condesa
Address: Michoacán 168
06170 México, D.F. Mexico
Phone: 55 5256 0950

#76
La Hacienda de los Morales
Cuisines: Mexican
Average price: Expensive
Area: Polanco
Address: Juan Vázquez Mella 525
11510 México, D.F. Mexico
Phone: 55 5096 3054

#77
Hiyoko Yakitori-Ya
Cuisines: Japanese
Average price: Expensive
Area: Cuauhtémoc
Address: Río Pánuco 132
06500 México, D.F. Mexico
Phone: 55 5207 0386

#78
Morimoto
Cuisines: Japanese
Average price: Exclusive
Area: Anzures, Polanco
Address: Mariano Escobedo 700
11590 México, D.F. Mexico
Phone: 55 5263 8888

#79
La Casa de Toño
Cuisines: Mexican
Average price: Inexpensive
Area: Del Valle
Address: Av. Cuauhtémoc 439
03020 México, D.F. Mexico
Phone: 55 5386 1125

#80
Los Panchos
Cuisines: Mexican
Average price: Modest
Area: Anzures
Address: Tolstoi 9
11590 México, D.F. Mexico
Phone: 55 5254 5430

#81
Pulquería Los Insurgentes
Cuisines: Mexican, Dive Bar
Average price: Modest
Area: Roma Norte
Address: Insurgentes Sur 226
06700 México, D.F. Mexico
Phone: 55 5207 0917

#82
El Rey del Marisco
Cuisines: Seafood
Average price: Expensive
Area: Condesa
Address: Av. Chapultepec 464
06700 México, D.F. Mexico
Phone: 55 5511 1696

#83
La Tecla
Cuisines: Mexican, Bar
Average price: Expensive
Area: Condesa
Address: Durgango 186
06700 México, D.F. Mexico
Phone: 55 5525 4920

#84
Fonda Fina
Cuisines: Mexican
Average price: Modest
Area: Condesa
Address: Medellin 79
06700 México, D.F. Mexico
Phone: 55 5208 3925

#85
El Maquech Púrpura
Cuisines: Mexican
Average price: Modest
Area: Narvarte
Address: Dr. José María Vértiz 808
03020 México, D.F. Mexico
Phone: 55 5590 9577

#86
La Palomiux
Cuisines: Mexican
Average price: Inexpensive
Area: Juárez
Address: Calle Lucerna 151
06600 México, D.F. Mexico
Phone: 55 4544 2899

#87
Henry Sailor
Cuisines: Seafood
Average price: Modest
Area: Narvarte
Address: Av. Universidad 281
03020 México, D.F. Mexico
Phone: 55 1107 6071

#88
Eric Kayser
Cuisines: French, Bakeries,
Breakfast & Brunch
Average price: Modest
Area: Juárez
Address: Paseo de la Reforma 408
06500 México, D.F. Mexico
Phone: 55 5207 4205

#89
Romita Comedor
Cuisines: Cocktail Bar, Mexican
Average price: Expensive
Area: Roma Norte
Address: Alvaro Obregón 49
06700 México, D.F. Mexico
Phone: 55 5525 8975

#90
Macelleria
Cuisines: Italian
Average price: Expensive
Area: Roma Norte
Address: Orizaba 127
06700 México, D.F. Mexico
Phone: 55 5564 0345

#91
Escarapela
Cuisines: Argentine
Average price: Modest
Area: Condesa
Address: Nuevo León 62
06140 México, D.F. Mexico
Phone: 55 5211 4444

#92
Salón Corona
Cuisines: Beer Bar, Mexican
Average price: Inexpensive
Area: Centro Sur
Address: Calle Gante 1
06000 México, D.F. Mexico
Phone: 55 5512 2024

#93
La Burguesa
Cuisines: Burgers
Average price: Modest
Area: Condesa
Address: Cozumel 67
06700 México, D.F. Mexico
Phone: 55 6272 7078

#94
El Rey de las Ahogadas
Cuisines: Mexican, Rotisserie Chicken
Average price: Inexpensive
Area: Del Valle
Address: Av. Coyoacán 360
03100 México, D.F. Mexico
Phone: 55 5523 4989

#95
El Cardenal
Cuisines: Mexican
Average price: Expensive
Area: San Ángel
Address: Av. de la Paz 32
01000 México, D.F. Mexico
Phone: 55 5550 0293

#96
La Chirindongueria
Cuisines: Spanish
Average price: Modest
Area: Centro Poniente
Address: Iturbide 31
06000 México, D.F. Mexico
Phone: 55 5510 1115

#97
Restaurante Escuela Zéfiro
Cuisines: Mexican
Average price: Expensive
Area: Centro Sur
Address: San Jerónimo 24
06010 México, D.F. Mexico
Phone: 55 5709 7983

#98
Salón Ríos
Cuisines: Dive Bar, Mexican, Cocktail Bar
Average price: Modest
Area: Cuauhtémoc
Address: Rio Lerma 218
06500 México, D.F. Mexico
Phone: 55 5207 5272

#99
Groove
Cuisines: Gastropubs
Average price: Modest
Area: Condesa
Address: Citlaltépetl 9
06170 México, D.F. Mexico
Phone: 55 5211 7526

#100
Pakaá
Cuisines: Mediterranean
Average price: Inexpensive
Area: San Rafael
Address: Francisco Díaz Covarrubias 36
06470 México, D.F. Mexico
Phone: 55 4444 1753

#101
Tacos Don Juan
Cuisines: Tacos
Average price: Inexpensive
Area: Condesa
Address: Atlixco 42
06760 México, D.F. Mexico
Phone: 55 5286 0816

#102
Puerto Madero
Cuisines: Argentine
Average price: Expensive
Area: Polanco
Address: Presidente Masaryk 110
11550 México, D.F. Mexico
Phone: 55 5545 6098

#103
Mezzo Mezzo
Cuisines: Italian
Average price: Modest
Area: Cuauhtémoc
Address: Río Neva 30 A
54124 México, D.F. Mexico
Phone: 99 162 28163

#104
La Casa de Toño
Cuisines: Mexican
Average price: Inexpensive
Area: Juárez
Address: Londres 144
06600 México, D.F. Mexico
Phone: 55 5386 1125

#105
Xampañería
Cuisines: Tapas/Small Plates, Cocktail Bar
Average price: Expensive
Area: Condesa
Address: Nuevo León 66
06170 México, D.F. Mexico
Phone: 55 4432 4073

#106
Niwa Daikoku
Cuisines: Japanese
Average price: Modest
Area: Coyoacán
Address: Londres 348
04100 México, D.F. Mexico
Phone: 55 5554 8980

#107
Yoma Noodle Bar
Cuisines: Ramen
Average price: Modest
Area: Nápoles
Address: Insurgentes Sur 623
03810 México, D.F. Mexico
Phone: 55 5523 2300

#108
La Taberna del Tio Chanclas
Cuisines: Spanish
Average price: Expensive
Area: Condesa
Address: Aguascalientes 206
06140 México, D.F. Mexico
Phone: 55 5264 3997

#109
Bellopuerto
Cuisines: Seafood
Average price: Expensive
Area: Polanco
Address: Calle Julio Verne 89
11560 México, D.F. Mexico
Phone: 55 5281 0980

#110
Patagonia Parilla de Campo
Cuisines: Steakhouse, Argentine
Average price: Expensive
Area: Condesa
Address: Campeche 345
06100 México, D.F. Mexico
Phone: 55 5211 8032

#111
Attenti
Cuisines: Italian, Spanish
Average price: Modest
Area: Cuauhtémoc
Address: Río Lerma 175
06500 México, D.F. Mexico
Phone: 55 5525 9341

#112
Taquería El Califa
Cuisines: Tacos
Average price: Modest
Area: Condesa
Address: Altata 22
06100 México, D.F. Mexico
Phone: 55 5271 7666

#113
Fonda Mayora
Cuisines: Mexican
Average price: Expensive
Area: Condesa
Address: Campeche 322
06100 México, D.F. Mexico
Phone: 55 5211 5953

#114
Los Amantes Café & Bistrot
Cuisines: Cafeteria, Bistros
Average price: Modest
Area: Coyoacán
Address: Felipe Carrillo Puerto 19
04000 México, D.F. Mexico
Phone: 55 7576 0946

#115
El Beso Huasteco
Cuisines: Mexican
Average price: Modest
Area: Roma Norte
Address: Calle Córdoba 146
06700 México, D.F. Mexico
Phone: 55 5264 1591

#116
El Rincón del Peribán
Cuisines:
Average price: Inexpensive
Area: Juárez
Address: Génova 75
06600 México, D.F. Mexico
Phone: 55 5207 6146

#117
Nonsolo Centro Histórico
Cuisines: Mexican
Average price: Modest
Area: Centro Sur
Address: Motolinía 37
06000 México, D.F. Mexico
Phone: 55 5512 0619

#118
Porco Rosso
Cuisines: American, Barbeque, Sandwiches
Average price: Modest
Area: Roma Norte
Address: Calle Zacatecas 102
06700 México, D.F. Mexico
Phone: 55 5264 4355

#119
Cine Tonalá
Cuisines: Cinema, Cefe, Bar
Average price: Modest
Area: Roma Sur
Address: Tonalá 261
06470 México, D.F. Mexico
Phone: 55 5264 4101

#120
Eno
Cuisines: Sandwiches, Salad
Average price: Modest
Area: Polanco
Address: Francisco Petrarca 258
11550 México, D.F. Mexico
Phone: 55 5531 8300

#121
El Hidalguense
Cuisines: Mexican
Average price: Modest
Area: Roma Sur
Address: Campeche 155
06760 México, D.F. Mexico
Phone: 55 5564 0538

#122
MIT Steak Bar
Cuisines: American, Steakhouse
Average price: Expensive
Area: Condesa
Address: Iztaccihuatl 36
06100 México, D.F. Mexico
Phone: 55 5264 1155

#123
La Casa del Pan Papálotl
Cuisines: Cafeteria
Average price: Inexpensive
Area: Coyoacán
Address: Av. México 25B
04100 México, D.F. Mexico
Phone: 55 3095 1767

#124
Cafetería del MUMEDI
Cuisines: Cafeteria
Average price: Modest
Area: Centro Sur
Address: Francisco I Madero 74
06000 México, D.F. Mexico
Phone: 55 5510 8609

#125
Astrid & Gastón
Cuisines: Peruvian
Average price: Exclusive
Area: Polanco
Address: Tennyson 117
11560 México, D.F. Mexico
Phone: 55 5282 2666

#126
Galanga Thai Kitchen
Cuisines: Thai
Average price: Modest
Area: Roma Norte
Address: Guanajuato 202
06700 México, D.F. Mexico
Phone: 55 6550 4492

#127
La Tlayudería
Cuisines: Oaxacan
Average price: Modest
Area: Roma Norte
Address: Calle Tonalá 155
06700 México, D.F. Mexico
Phone: 55 4751 1951

#128
Barro Negro
Cuisines: Oaxacan
Average price: Expensive
Area: Polanco
Address: Av. Moliére 48
11550 México, D.F. Mexico
Phone: 55 5280 0584

#129
Casa Merlos
Cuisines: Pueblan
Average price: Expensive
Area: Observatorio
Address: Victoriano Zepeda 80
11860 México, D.F. Mexico
Phone: 55 5277 4360

#130
La Buena Barra
Cuisines: Mexican
Average price: Exclusive
Area: Polanco
Address: Aristóteles 124
11550 México, D.F. Mexico
Phone: 55 5280 6699

#131
Café Toscano
Cuisines: Cafeteria
Average price: Modest
Area: Roma Norte
Address: Calle Orizaba 42
06700 México, D.F. Mexico
Phone: 55 5533 5444

#132
Bar La Ópera
Cuisines: Mexican, Bar, Seafood
Average price: Modest
Area: Centro Sur
Address: Av. 5 de Mayo 10
06010 México, D.F. Mexico
Phone: 55 5512 8959

#133
Nadefo
Cuisines: Korean
Average price: Expensive
Area: Juárez
Address: Liverpool 183
06600 México, D.F. Mexico
Phone: 55 5525 0351

#134
Don Toribio
Cuisines: Mexican
Average price: Modest
Area: Centro Sur
Address: Bolívar 31
03440 México, D.F. Mexico
Phone: 55 5510 9198

#135
Trattoria Toscana
Cuisines: Italian
Average price: Modest
Area: Juárez
Address: Copenhague 29
06600 México, D.F. Mexico
Phone: 55 5511 9704

#136
Eloise, Chic Cuisine
Cuisines: Modern European
Average price: Exclusive
Area: San Ángel
Address: Revolución 1521
01000 México, D.F. Mexico
Phone: 55 5550 1692

#137
Eno
Cuisines: Cafeteria
Average price: Modest
Area: Las Lomas
Address: Explanada 730
11000 México, D.F. Mexico
Phone: 55 5202 9808

#138
Pepe Coyotes
Cuisines: Mexican
Average price: Modest
Area: Coyoacán
Address: Av. Miguel Hidalgo 297
04100 México, D.F. Mexico
Phone: 55 5659 8902

#139
Maison Belen
Cuisines: Cafeteria, French, Desserts
Average price: Modest
Area: Polanco
Address: Emilio Castelar 31
11550 México, D.F. Mexico
Phone: 55 5280 3756

#140
Chilpa
Cuisines: Tacos
Average price: Inexpensive
Area: Condesa
Address: Chilpancingo 35
06100 México, D.F. Mexico
Phone: 55 5264 4976

#141
Broka Bistrot
Cuisines: Bistros
Average price: Modest
Area: Roma Norte
Address: Zacatecas 126
06700 México, D.F. Mexico
Phone: 55 4437 4285

#142
Taquería Los Parados
Cuisines: Tacos
Average price: Inexpensive
Area: Roma Sur
Address: Monterrey 333
06760 México, D.F. Mexico
Phone: 55 5264 7138

#143
El Sabor del Tiempo
Cuisines: Cefe
Average price: Inexpensive
Area: Nápoles
Address: Altadena 8
03810 México, D.F. Mexico
Phone: 55 5523 1802

#144
El Huequito
Cuisines: Tacos
Average price: Expensive
Area: Centro Sur
Address: Bolívar 58
06000 México, D.F. Mexico
Phone: 55 5521 0207

#145
Tacontento
Cuisines: Tacos
Average price: Modest
Area: Juárez
Address: Londres 91
06600 México, D.F. Mexico
Phone: 55 5514 8073

#146
Bonito Pop Food
Cuisines: American
Average price: Expensive
Area: Condesa
Address: Av. Nuevo León 103
06100 México, D.F. Mexico
Phone: 55 5286 6169

#147
The Comrade
Cuisines: Cocktail Bar, Mediterranean
Average price: Expensive
Area: Polanco
Address: Emilio Castelar 149
11550 México, D.F. Mexico
Phone: 55 5280 2195

#148
Fonda El Morral
Cuisines: Mexican
Average price: Modest
Area: Coyoacán
Address: Allende 2
04100 México, D.F. Mexico
Phone: 55 5554 0298

#149
La Taberna del León
Cuisines:
Average price: Exclusive
Area: San Ángel
Address: Altamirano 46
01000 México, D.F. Mexico
Phone: 55 5616 2110

#150
Parrilla Leonesa
Cuisines: Cefe
Average price: Expensive
Area: Centro Sur
Address: Bolívar 29 A
06010 México, D.F. Mexico
Phone: 55 5510 0172

#151
El Huequito
Cuisines: Tacos
Average price: Modest
Area: Condesa
Address: Bajo Puente, Local 4 Esq. Juan
Escutia. 11850 México, D.F. Mexico
Phone: 55 5553 7136

#152
El Jarocho
Cuisines: Tacos
Average price: Modest
Area: Roma Sur
Address: Manzanillo 50
06760 México, D.F. Mexico
Phone: 55 5584 8008

#153
Frutos Prohibidos y Otros Placeres
Cuisines: Juice Bar & Smoothies,
Sandwiches, Salad
Average price: Modest
Area: Juárez
Address: Toledo 4
06600 México, D.F. Mexico
Phone: 55 5207 1717

#154
El Antiguo Edén
Cuisines: Arabian
Average price: Expensive
Area: Centro Sur
Address: Venustiano Carranza 148
06000 México, D.F. Mexico
Phone: 55 5542 2320

#155
Takenoya
Cuisines: Japanese
Average price: Expensive
Area: Polanco
Address: Moliere 313
11550 México, D.F. Mexico
Phone: 55 5545 7565

#156
Prego
Cuisines: Italian, Wine Bar
Average price: Expensive
Area: Polanco
Address: Alejandro Dumas 10
11560 México, D.F. Mexico
Phone: 55 5281 2637

#157
Piantao
Cuisines: Argentine
Average price: Exclusive
Area: Tlalpan
Address: Av. San Fernando 649
14060 México, D.F. Mexico
Phone: 55 5424 0012

#158
Restaurante Centro Castellano
Cuisines: Spanish, Bar
Average price: Expensive
Area: Centro Sur
Address: Uruguay 16
06000 México, D.F. Mexico
Phone: 55 5518 6080

#159
Taqueria los Gueros
Cuisines: Tacos
Average price: Inexpensive
Area: Jardín Balbuena
Address: Lorenzo Boturini No. 1702
15980 México, D.F. Mexico
Phone: 55 5764 4126

#160
La Casa de las Enchiladas
Cuisines: Mexican
Average price: Modest
Area: Escandón
Address: Bajío 374, Roma Sur
06100 México, D.F. Mexico
Phone: 55 5276 9841

#161
De Mar a Mar
Cuisines: Seafood
Average price: Expensive
Area: Juárez
Address: Niza 13
06600 México, D.F. Mexico
Phone: 55 5207 5730

#162
La Casa de Toño
Cuisines: Mexican
Average price: Inexpensive
Area: Santa María la Ribera
Address: Calle Sabino 166
06400 México, D.F. Mexico
Phone: 55 6273 6049

#163
El Turix
Cuisines: Yucatan, Tacos, Street Vendor
Average price: Inexpensive
Area: Polanco
Address: Emilio Castelar 212
11550 México, D.F. Mexico
Phone: 55 5280 6449

#164
Fogonazo
Cuisines: Tacos
Average price: Modest
Area: Condesa
Address: Culiacán 51
06100 México, D.F. Mexico
Phone: 55 5913 5383

#165
Tacos Don Frank
Cuisines: Tacos
Average price: Inexpensive
Area: Del Valle
Address: Torres Adalid 1353
03020 México, D.F. Mexico
Phone: 52 552 39101

#166
3D LAB
Cuisines: Cafeteria, Coffee & Tea
Average price: Modest
Area: Roma Norte
Address: Av. Tonalá 89
06700 México, D.F. Mexico
Phone: 55 5264 1107

#167
Los Almendros
Cuisines: Mexican
Average price: Expensive
Area: Polanco
Address: Campos Elíseos 164
11580 México, D.F. Mexico
Phone: 55 5531 6646

#168
Rincón Libanés
Cuisines: Coffee & Tea, Lebanese
Average price: Inexpensive
Area: Cuauhtémoc
Address: Río Tigris 78-B
06500 México, D.F. Mexico
Phone: 55 5525 1905

#169
Tamales Teresita
Cuisines: Tamales
Average price: Inexpensive
Area: Buenavista
Address: Niños Héroes 147
06300 México, D.F. Mexico
Phone: 55 5526 1779

#170
Pulquería Duelistas
Cuisines: Dive Bar, Mexican
Average price: Inexpensive
Area: Centro Poniente
Address: Aranda 28
06000 México, D.F. Mexico
Phone: 55 1394 0958

#171
Taqueria El Abanico
Cuisines: Tacos
Average price: Inexpensive
Area: Tránsito
Address: Francisco J. Clavijero 226
04320 México, D.F. Mexico
Phone: 55 5740 2813

#172
Xanat Bistro & Terrace
Cuisines: Mexican
Average price: Expensive
Area: Polanco
Address: Andrés Bello 29
11550 México, D.F. Mexico
Phone: 55 5999 0066

#173
J By José Andrés
Cuisines: Spanish, Cocktail Bar
Average price: Expensive
Area: Polanco
Address: Campos Elíseos 252
11560 México, D.F. Mexico
Phone: 55 9138 1818

#174
Lampuga
Cuisines: Seafood
Average price: Expensive
Area: Condesa
Address: Ometusco 1
06100 México, D.F. Mexico
Phone: 55 5286 1525

#175
Café de Raíz
Cuisines: Cafeteria
Average price: Inexpensive
Area: Roma Norte
Address: Mérida 132
06700 México, D.F. Mexico
Phone: 55 5584 8847

#176
Delirio
Cuisines: Delicatessen, French
Average price: Modest
Area: Roma Norte
Address: Monterrey 116 B
06700 México, D.F. Mexico
Phone: 55 5584 0870

#177
Maison Artemisia
Cuisines: Cocktail Bar, French, Piano Bar
Average price: Expensive
Area: Roma Norte
Address: Tonalá 23
06700 México, D.F. Mexico
Phone: 55 6303 2471

#178
Taquitos Frontera
Cuisines: Tacos
Average price: Inexpensive
Area: Roma Norte
Address: Álvaro Obregón 25
06700 México, D.F. Mexico
Phone: 55 4632 1261

#179
Los Bisquets Bisquets Obregón
Cuisines: Breakfast & Brunch, Mexican
Average price: Inexpensive
Area: Centro Sur
Address: Av. Francisco I. Madero 29-31
06000 México, D.F. Mexico
Phone: 55 5510 4032

#180
Non Solo
Cuisines: Italian, Mediterranean
Average price: Modest
Area: Roma Norte
Address: Av. Álvaro Obregón 130
06700 México, D.F. Mexico
Phone: 55 5574 8577

#181
Yume
Cuisines: Antiques, Cafeteria
Average price: Modest
Area: Escandón
Address: Calle Sindicalismo S/N
11800 México, D.F. Mexico
Phone: 55 2614 2376

#182
Fiebre de Malta
Cuisines: Gastropubs, Beer Bar
Average price: Modest
Area: Cuauhtémoc
Address: Río Lerma 156
06500 México, D.F. Mexico
Phone: 55 5207 0491

#183
Brassi
Cuisines: Cefe
Average price: Expensive
Area: Polanco
Address: Virgilio 8 11560 México, D.F.
Mexico
Phone: 55 5281 4357

#184
Belmondo
Cuisines: Salad, Cocktail Bar, Sandwiches
Average price: Expensive
Area: Polanco
Address: Emilio Castelar 171
11540 México, D.F. Mexico
Phone: 55 5280 3221

#185
Pleno
Cuisines: Mexican
Average price: Expensive
Area: Condesa
Address: Calle Citlatepetl 23
06100 México, D.F. Mexico
Phone: 55 6719 6073

#186
Danubio
Cuisines: Spanish, International
Average price: Expensive
Area: Centro Sur
Address: República de Uruguay 3
06000 México, D.F. Mexico
Phone: 55 5512 0912

#187
Cabrera 7
Cuisines: Mexican, Bar, Seafood
Average price: Modest
Area: Roma Norte
Address: Plaza Luis Cabrera 7
06700 México, D.F. Mexico
Phone: 55 5264 4531

#188
Surasang
Cuisines: Korean
Average price: Modest
Area: Juárez
Address: Varsovia 15
06600 México, D.F. Mexico
Phone: 55 5511 7929

#189
Tacos Gus
Cuisines: Tacos
Average price: Inexpensive
Area: Condesa
Address: Ometusco 56
06100 México, D.F. Mexico
Phone: 55 5271 6090

#190
Las Musas de PapáSibarita
Cuisines: Gastropubs, Italian, Mexican
Average price: Modest
Area: Roma Norte
Address: Orizaba 218
06760 México, D.F. Mexico
Phone: 55 1054 6169

#191
Quebracho
Cuisines: Argentine, Steakhouse
Average price: Expensive
Area: Juárez
Address: Hamburgo 313
06600 México, D.F. Mexico
Phone: 55 5256 4790

#192
Burgers by Buba
Cuisines: Burgers
Average price: Modest
Area: Juárez
Address: Londres 164
06600 México, D.F. Mexico
Phone: 55 5208 2502

#193
El Cordobés
Cuisines: Cafeteria
Average price: Inexpensive
Area: Centro Poniente
Address: Ayuntamiento 18
06000 México, D.F. Mexico
Phone: 55 5512 5545

#194
Licorería Limantour
Cuisines: Cefe, Cocktail Bar
Average price: Modest
Area: Polanco
Address: Oscar Wilde 9
11560 México, D.F. Mexico
Phone: 55 5280 1299

#195
Las Tlayudas
Cuisines: Oaxacan
Average price: Modest
Area: Roma Norte
Address: Av. San Luis Potosí 13
06700 México, D.F. Mexico
Phone: 55 6379 2496

#196
Mexsi Bocu
Cuisines: Mexican, French
Average price: Expensive
Area: Condesa
Address: Durango 359
06700 México, D.F. Mexico
Phone: 55 3099 4920

#197
Mazurka
Cuisines: Polish
Average price: Expensive
Area: Nápoles
Address: Calle Nueva York 150
03810 México, D.F. Mexico
Phone: 55 5523 8811

#198
El Lago
Cuisines: Breakfast & Brunch
Average price: Expensive
Area: Chapultepec 2a Sección
Address: Lago Mayor
11580 México, D.F. Mexico
Phone: 55 5515 9585

#199
El Chalet
Cuisines: Tacos
Average price: Modest
Area: Del Valle
Address: Calz. Obrero Mundial 225
03100 México, D.F. Mexico
Phone: 55 5536 3602

#200
Tori Tori
Cuisines: Japanese
Average price: Expensive
Area: Polanco
Address: Anatole France 71-B
11560 México, D.F. Mexico
Phone: 55 5280 8067

#201
Centenario 107
Cuisines: Pizza, Dive Bar
Average price: Modest
Area: Coyoacán
Address: Centenario 107
04100 México, D.F. Mexico
Phone: 55 4752 6369

#202
Papa Guapa
Cuisines: Cafeteria
Average price: Modest
Area: Condesa
Address: Av Oaxaca 80
06700 México, D.F. Mexico
Phone: 55 5511 6680

#203
Sesame
Cuisines: Asian Fusion
Average price: Expensive
Area: Roma Norte
Address: Colima 183
06700 México, D.F. Mexico
Phone: 55 5207 7471

#204
Lardo
Cuisines: Breakfast & Brunch,
French, Cafeteria
Average price: Modest
Area: Condesa
Address: Agustín Melgar 6
06140 México, D.F. Mexico
Phone: 55 5211 7731

#205
George
Cuisines: Mediterranean
Average price: Expensive
Area: Polanco
Address: Presidente Masaryk 192
11550 México, D.F. Mexico
Phone: 55 5281 3515

#206
Bistrot M
Cuisines: Cefe
Average price: Modest
Area: Del Valle
Address: Amores 1403
03100 México, D.F. Mexico
Phone: 55 5688 1082

#207
Uelik
Cuisines: Diner
Average price: Modest
Area: Condesa
Address: Parras 15
06140 México, D.F. Mexico
Phone: 55 6585 8103

#208
Cancino
Cuisines: Pizza, Bar, Italian
Average price: Modest
Area: Condesa
Address: Plaza de Villa Madrid 13
06700 México, D.F. Mexico
Phone: 55 6650 8598

#209
Ouzeria
Cuisines: Bar, Greek, Mediterranean
Average price: Expensive
Area: Polanco
Address: Calle Julio Verne 95
11500 México, D.F. Mexico
Phone: 55 5292 8639

#210
Angelopolitano
Cuisines: Candy Store, Mexican, Sandwiches
Average price: Modest
Area: Condesa
Address: Puebla 371
06700 México, D.F. Mexico
Phone: 55 6391 2121

#211
Librería Porrúa
Cuisines: BookStore, Cafeteria
Average price: Modest
Area: Chapultepec 1a Sección
Address: Bosque de Chapultepec
11560 México, D.F. Mexico
Phone: 55 5212 2241

#212
La Chicha
Cuisines:
Average price: Modest
Area: Roma Norte
Address: Orizaba 171 Col. Roma
06700 México, D.F. Mexico
Phone: 55 5574 6625

#213
El Rincón de la Lechuza
Cuisines: Mexican
Average price: Modest
Area: Florida
Address: Av. Miguel Ángel de Quevedo 34
01050 México, D.F. Mexico
Phone: 55 5661 5911

#214
Linneo
Cuisines: Cefe, Cocktail Bar
Average price: Modest
Area: Condesa
Address: Avenida Michoacán 121
06140 México, D.F. Mexico
Phone: 55 6553 3582

#215
Deigo
Cuisines: Sushi Bar, Japanese
Average price: Expensive
Area: Del Valle
Address: Pestalozzi 1238
03100 México, D.F. Mexico
Phone: 55 5605 6317

#216
Las Ramonas
Cuisines: Mexican
Average price: Modest
Area: Santa María la Ribera
Address: Jaime Torres Bodet 220
06400 México, D.F. Mexico
Phone: 55 5541 2567

#217
Havanna
Cuisines: Cafeteria
Average price: Modest
Area: Polanco
Address: Presidente Masaryk 76
11550 México, D.F. Mexico
Phone: 55 5254 2609

#218
L' Encanto de Lola
Cuisines: Delis, Mexican
Average price: Modest
Area: San Ángel
Address: Amargura 14
01000 México, D.F. Mexico
Phone: 55 5550 8429

#219
Restaurante Los Machetes de Amparito
Cuisines: Mexican
Average price: Inexpensive
Area: Buenavista
Address: Héroes #192
06300 México, D.F. Mexico
Phone: 55 5526 4028

#220
Las Chalupitas
Cuisines: Pueblan
Average price: Modest
Area: Condesa
Address: Alfonso Reyes 275
06140 México, D.F. Mexico
Phone: 55 5515 6479

#221
Tacos Charly
Cuisines: Tacos
Average price: Inexpensive
Area: Tlalpan
Address: Av. San Fernando 195
14050 México, D.F. Mexico
Phone: 55 5606 2824

#222
Falafelito
Cuisines: Arabian, Vegetarian
Average price: Inexpensive
Area: Coyoacán
Address: Malitzin165
04100 México, D.F. Mexico
Phone: 55 6391 1007

#223
Bar de La Teatrería
Cuisines: Modern European, Lounge
Average price: Expensive
Area: Roma Norte
Address: Tabasco 152
06700 México, D.F. Mexico
Phone: 55 5208 0205

#224
El Bajío
Cuisines: Mexican
Average price: Modest
Area: Juárez
Address: Av. Paseo de la Reforma 222
06600 México, D.F. Mexico
Phone: 55 5511 9117

#225
Catamundi
Cuisines: Bar, Mexican
Average price: Expensive
Area: Polanco
Address: Alejandro Dumas 97
11550 México, D.F. Mexico
Phone: 55 5280 6681

#226
Zapote
Cuisines: Mediterranean, Italian
Average price: Expensive
Area: Roma Norte
Address: Guanajuato 138
06760 México, D.F. Mexico
Phone: 55 6391 6089

#227
Buenas Migas
Cuisines: Mexican, Mediterranean
Average price: Modest
Area: Del Valle
Address: Nicolás San Juan 251 C
03100 México, D.F. Mexico
Phone: 55 5638 0957

#228
Las Mercedes
Cuisines: Mexican, Seafood, Steakhouse
Average price: Modest
Area: Anzures
Address: Darwin 113
06720 México, D.F. Mexico
Phone: 55 5254 5044

#229
Nueve Nueve
Cuisines: Mexican, Cafeteria
Average price: Expensive
Area: Roma Norte
Address: Av. Álvaro Obregón 99
06700 México, D.F. Mexico
Phone: 55 5525 9795

#230
Fonda Garufa
Cuisines: Steakhouse, Pizza
Average price: Expensive
Area: Condesa
Address: Av. Michoacán 93
06140 México, D.F. Mexico
Phone: 55 5286 8295

#231
Kolobok
Cuisines: Russian
Average price: Modest
Area: Narvarte
Address: Av. Universidad 538
03650 México, D.F. Mexico
Phone: 55 5604 4091

#232
Anderson's
Cuisines: Pubs, International
Average price: Expensive
Area: Juárez
Address: Paseo de la Reforma 382
06600 México, D.F. Mexico
Phone: 55 5208 2150

#233
El Auténtico Pato Manila
Cuisines: Fast Food, Chinese
Average price: Modest
Area: Condesa
Address: Culiacán 91
06100 México, D.F. Mexico
Phone: 55 6798 8351

#234
Torobi
Cuisines: Japanese
Average price: Expensive
Area: Polanco
Address: Alfredo Musset 3
11550 México, D.F. Mexico
Phone: 55 5282 2020

#235
Sonora Grill
Cuisines: Barbeque, Italian, Mexican
Average price: Expensive
Area: General Anaya
Address: Av. Coyoacán 1955
03330 México, D.F. Mexico
Phone: 55 5604 1571

#236
EL JOLGORIO
Cuisines:
Average price: Modest
Area: Condesa
Address: Plaza Villa De Madrid 9, Col. Roma
06700 México, D.F. Mexico
Phone: 55 5511 9570

#237
Los Chamos
Cuisines: Latin American, Burgers
Average price: Modest
Area: Narvarte
Address: Diagonal San Antonio 1689-C
04480 México, D.F. Mexico
Phone: 55 5519 3759

#238
Alipus Endémico
Cuisines: Oaxacan, Bar
Average price: Modest
Area: Condesa
Address: Alfonso Reyes 224
06100 México, D.F. Mexico
Phone: 55 5211 6845

#239
Corazón de Maguey
Cuisines: Eastern Mexican,
Yucatan, Oaxacan
Average price: Expensive
Area: Coyoacán
Address: Plaza Jardín Centenario 9-A
04000 México, D.F. Mexico
Phone: 55 5659 3165

#240
Kaye
Cuisines: Mexican, Seafood
Average price: Expensive
Area: Condesa
Address: Alfonso Reyes 108
06170 México, D.F. Mexico
Phone: 55 7045 1722

#241
La Cervecería de Barrio
Cuisines: Seafood
Average price: Modest
Area: Condesa
Address: Durango 192
06700 México, D.F. Mexico
Phone: 55 5533 7674

#242
Tamales Emporio San Rafael
Cuisines: Tamales
Average price: Modest
Area: San Rafael
Address: Manuel María Contreras 18-A
06470 México, D.F. Mexico
Phone: 55 5546 2134

#243
El Tizoncito
Cuisines: Mexican
Average price: Modest
Area: Condesa
Address: Tamaulipas 122
06140 México, D.F. Mexico
Phone: 55 5286 2117

#244
El Cielo de Cortés
Cuisines: Cefe, Bar
Average price: Expensive
Area: Buenavista
Address: Av. Hidalgo 85
06300 México, D.F. Mexico
Phone: 55 5518 2181

#245
Havre
Cuisines: Pizza, Italian, Cocktail Bar
Average price: Modest
Area: Juárez
Address: Havre 64
06600 México, D.F. Mexico
Phone: 55 5207 4398

#246
Las Jirafas y la Mula
Cuisines: Mexican
Average price: Inexpensive
Area: Santa María la Ribera
Address: Doctor Atl 221
06400 México, D.F. Mexico
Phone: 55 5547 6907

#247
La Casa de los Abuelos
Cuisines: Mexican
Average price: Modest
Area: Juárez
Address: Hamburgo 87
06600 México, D.F. Mexico
Phone: 55 5207 5439

#248
Il Ritrovo
Cuisines: Italian
Average price: Modest
Area: Juárez
Address: Copenhage 4
06600 México, D.F. Mexico
Phone: 55 5533 6449

#249
Hostería de Santo Domingo
Cuisines: Mexican
Average price: Modest
Area: Centro Norte
Address: Calle Belisario Domínguez 72
06010 México, D.F. Mexico
Phone: 55 5526 5276

#250
Central de Brazil Churrascaria
Cuisines: Brazilian, Steakhouse
Average price: Exclusive
Area: San Ángel
Address: Av. de la Paz 48
01000 México, D.F. Mexico
Phone: 55 5550 1713

#251
Ela Gyros
Cuisines: Greek
Average price: Inexpensive
Area: Narvarte
Address: La Morena 1112
03020 México, D.F. Mexico
Phone: 55 5019 1913

#252
Las Tinajas
Cuisines: Spanish
Average price: Inexpensive
Area: Cuauhtémoc
Address: Plaza Melchor Ocampo 14
06500 México, D.F. Mexico
Phone: 55 5207 8899

#253
Don Chui
Cuisines: Chinese
Average price: Modest
Area: Polanco
Address: Virgilio 40
11550 México, D.F. Mexico
Phone: 55 5281 0440

#254
La Poblanita
Cuisines: Mexican
Average price: Modest
Area: San Miguel Chapultepec
Address: Calle Luis G. Vieyra 12
11850 México, D.F. Mexico
Phone: 55 2614 3314

#255
La Pause
Cuisines: Mexican
Average price: Modest
Area: Coyoacán
Address: Av. Francisco Sosa 287
04010 México, D.F. Mexico
Phone: 55 5658 6780

#256
Los Danzantes
Cuisines: Mexican, Bar
Average price: Expensive
Area: Coyoacán
Address: Jardín Centenario 12
04100 México, D.F. Mexico
Phone: 55 5554 1213

#257
Tortas Robles
Cuisines: Mexican
Average price: Modest
Area: Centro Poniente
Address: Colón 1
06000 México, D.F. Mexico
Phone: 55 5521 1624

#258
Pizza del Perro Negro
Cuisines: Pizza
Average price: Modest
Area: Centro Norte
Address: Donceles 66
06060 México, D.F. Mexico
Phone: 55 5512 5490

#259
Rincón Argentino
Cuisines: Argentine
Average price: Expensive
Area: Polanco
Address: Presidente Masaryk 177
11570 México, D.F. Mexico
Phone: 99 188 81357

#260
Casa Portuguesa
Cuisines: Portuguese
Average price: Exclusive
Area: Polanco
Address: Emilio Castelar 111
11560 México, D.F. Mexico
Phone: 55 5280 6885

#261
Volver Co
Cuisines: Burgers, Vegan, Organic Store
Average price: Modest
Area: Roma Norte
Address: Chihuahua 93
06700 México, D.F. Mexico
Phone: 55 5264 8731

#262
Temporal
Cuisines: Cefe, Bar
Average price: Modest
Area: Condesa
Address: Saltillo 1
06140 México, D.F. Mexico
Phone: 55 5211 5477

#263
La Casa de las Enchiladas
Cuisines: Breakfast & Brunch
Average price: Modest
Area: Cuauhtémoc
Address: Calle Río Lerma 257 A
06500 México, D.F. Mexico
Phone: 55 5207 6760

#264
Caldos D' Leo
Cuisines: Mexican
Average price: Modest
Area: Polanco
Address: Av. Ejército Nacional 1014
11520 México, D.F. Mexico
Phone: 55 5557 6760

#265
La Buenavida
Cuisines: Mexican, Diner
Average price: Inexpensive
Area: Roma Norte
Address: Mérida 92
06700 México, D.F. Mexico
Phone: 55 5511 8293

#266
Beluga
Cuisines: Gastropubs
Average price: Modest
Area: Escandón
Address: Progreso 92
11800 México, D.F. Mexico
Phone: 55 2614 8124

#267
Tacos la Palmera
Cuisines: Tacos
Average price: Inexpensive
Area: Juárez
Address: Hamburgo 259
06600 México, D.F. Mexico
Phone: 55 5533 8377

#268
50 Friends
Cuisines: Cefe
Average price: Expensive
Area: Juárez
Address: Paseo de la Reforma 342
06500 México, D.F. Mexico
Phone: 55 5207 7762

#269
Cassius
Cuisines: Tapas/Small Plates,
Mexican, Mediterranean
Average price: Expensive
Area: Roma Norte
Address: Orizaba 76
06700 México, D.F. Mexico
Phone: 55 6383 7050

#270
Café El Jarocho
Cuisines: Cafeteria
Average price: Inexpensive
Area: Centro Norte
Address: San Ildefonso 38
06020 México, D.F. Mexico
Phone: 55 5512 1916

#271
Ermitaño
Cuisines: Pizza
Average price: Modest
Area: Tabacalera
Address: Insurgentes Centro 16 C
06030 México, D.F. Mexico
Phone: 55 5546 0866

#272
El botellón
Cuisines: Spanish
Average price: Expensive
Area: Condesa
Address: Tamaulipas 106
06100 México, D.F. Mexico
Phone: 55 6395 4444

#273
Cafebrería El Péndulo
Cuisines: BookStore, Cafeteria
Average price: Modest
Area: Roma Norte
Address: Álvaro Obregón 86
06700 México, D.F. Mexico
Phone: 55 5574 7034

#274
El Fogoncito
Cuisines: Mexican
Average price: Modest
Area: Anzures
Address: Leibnitz 55
11590 México, D.F. Mexico
Phone: 55 5531 6497

#275
Pulquería La Nuclear
Cuisines: Dive Bar, Mexican
Average price: Inexpensive
Area: Juárez
Address: Querétaro 161
06700 México, D.F. Mexico
Phone: 55 5574 5367

#276
La Casa del Bauce
Cuisines: Mexican
Average price: Inexpensive
Area: Narvarte
Address: Avenida Universidad 412
03020 México, D.F. Mexico
Phone: 55 5543 9887

#277
Las Costillas de San Luis
Cuisines: Mexican
Average price: Inexpensive
Area: Roma Norte
Address: San Luis Potosí 129
06700 México, D.F. Mexico
Phone: 99 160 84932

#278
La Bodeguita del Medio
Cuisines: Bar, Cuban
Average price: Expensive
Area: Condesa
Address: Cozumel 37
06700 México, D.F. Mexico
Phone: 55 5553 0411

#279
Restaurante Los Tacos
Cuisines: Mexican
Average price: Modest
Area: Centro Sur
Address: República de Uruguay 117
06000 México, D.F. Mexico
Phone: 55 5522 8570

#280
Dulcinea
Cuisines: Seafood, Mexican
Average price: Expensive
Area: Polanco
Address: Oscar Wilde 29
11560 México, D.F. Mexico
Phone: 55 5280 8909

#281
Café Passmar
Cuisines: Cafeteria, Coffee & Tea
Average price: Inexpensive
Area: Del Valle
Address: Adolfo Prieto 250
03100 México, D.F. Mexico
Phone: 55 5669 1994

#282
Cafebrería El Péndulo
Cuisines: BookStore
Average price: Modest
Area: Polanco
Address: Alejandro Dumas 81
11560 México, D.F. Mexico
Phone: 55 5280 4111

#283
Nibelungengarten
Cuisines: German
Average price: Modest
Area: Narvarte
Address: Dr. José Ma. Vertíz 1024
03600 México, D.F. Mexico
Phone: 55 5609 1309

#284
Ivoire
Cuisines: French
Average price: Expensive
Area: Polanco
Address: Emilio Castelar 95
11560 México, D.F. Mexico
Phone: 55 5280 0477

#285
The Capital Grille
Cuisines: Steakhouse
Average price: Expensive
Area: Juárez
Address: Havre 30
06600 México, D.F. Mexico
Phone: 55 5207 8358

#286
Tandoor
Cuisines: Indian, Pakistani
Average price: Expensive
Area: Anzures
Address: Copérnico 156
11590 México, D.F. Mexico
Phone: 55 5203 0045

#287
La Jersey
Cuisines: Delicatessen, Delis, Meat Shop
Average price: Expensive
Area: Centro Poniente
Address: Ernesto Pugibet 21
06070 México, D.F. Mexico
Phone: 55 5510 4374

#288
Puebla 109
Cuisines: Cocktail Bar, Mediterranean
Average price: Expensive
Area: Roma Norte
Address: Puebla 109
06700 México, D.F. Mexico
Phone: 55 6389 7333

#289
Johnny Rockets
Cuisines: American, Burgers
Average price: Modest
Area: Del Valle
Address: Parroquia 194
03100 México, D.F. Mexico
Phone: 55 5627 8448

#290
Vapiano Reforma
Cuisines: Italian
Average price: Modest
Area: Juárez
Address: Paseo de la Reforma 250
06600 México, D.F. Mexico
Phone: 55 5207 3929

#291
Mariscos Puerto Condesa
Cuisines: Seafood
Average price: Modest
Area: Condesa
Address: Pachuca 96
06140 México, D.F. Mexico
Phone: 55 5256 4483

#292
The Melting Pot
Cuisines: Fondue
Average price: Expensive
Area: Pedregal
Address: Av. de las Fuentes 425
14410 México, D.F. Mexico
Phone: 55 5280 5220

#293
Villa María
Cuisines: Mexican
Average price: Expensive
Area: Polanco
Address: Homero 704
11550 México, D.F. Mexico
Phone: 55 5203 0306

#294
El Farolito
Cuisines: Tacos
Average price: Expensive
Area: Condesa
Address: Altata 19
06100 México, D.F. Mexico
Phone: 55 5273 7297

#295
La Embajada Jarocha
Cuisines: Cefe
Average price: Modest
Area: Roma Norte
Address: Zacatecas 138
06700 México, D.F. Mexico
Phone: 55 5584 2570

#296
Restaurante Condesa DF
Cuisines: French, Cocktail Bar
Average price: Expensive
Area: Condesa
Address: Veracruz 102
06140 México, D.F. Mexico
Phone: 55 5282 2199

#297
La Tonina
Cuisines: Northern Mexican
Average price: Modest
Area: San Rafael
Address: Serapio Rendón 27
06470 México, D.F. Mexico
Phone: 55 5912 0366

#298
Mi Mu Cafe
Cuisines:
Average price: Modest
Area: Roma Norte
Address: Chihuahua 93 B
06700 México, D.F. Mexico
Phone: 55 5264 8731

#299
La Polar
Cuisines: Mexican
Average price: Modest
Area: San Rafael
Address: Guillermo Prieto 129
06470 México, D.F. Mexico
Phone: 55 5546 5066

#300
Café Toscano
Cuisines: Cafeteria
Average price: Modest
Area: Roma Norte
Address: Orizaba 145
06700 México, D.F. Mexico
Phone: 55 6731 5131

#301
La Zaranda
Cuisines: Seafood, Mexican
Average price: Expensive
Area: Condesa
Address: Plaza Villa de Madrid 17
06700 México, D.F. Mexico
Phone: 55 6726 4077

#302
Carbonvino
Cuisines: Mexican
Average price: Expensive
Area: Condesa
Address: Tamaulipas 51
06140 México, D.F. Mexico
Phone: 55 5286 0657

#303
Dulce Patria
Cuisines: Mexican
Average price: Exclusive
Area: Polanco
Address: Anatole France 100
11550 México, D.F. Mexico
Phone: 55 3300 3999

#304
Agapi Mu
Cuisines: Greek
Average price: Expensive
Area: Condesa
Address: Alfonso Reyes 96
06170 México, D.F. Mexico
Phone: 55 5286 1384

#305
Mythos
Cuisines: Greek
Average price: Expensive
Area: Polanco
Address: Isaac Newton 7
11550 México, D.F. Mexico
Phone: 55 5282 1372

#306
La Quimera
Cuisines: Mexican
Average price: Modest
Area: Tabacalera
Address: Plaza de la República y Ezequiel
Montes 06030 México, D.F. Mexico
Phone: 55 5535 2208

#307
Don Asado
Cuisines: Steakhouse
Average price: Modest
Area: Del Valle
Address: Parroquia 906
03100 México, D.F. Mexico
Phone: 55 5524 9143

#308
Maque
Cuisines: Bakeries, Breakfast & Brunch
Average price: Modest
Area: Polanco
Address: Emilio Castelar 209
11560 México, D.F. Mexico
Phone: 55 5281 6429

#309
Sonora Grill Prime
Cuisines: Steakhouse, Bar
Average price: Expensive
Area: Condesa
Address: Durango 205
06700 México, D.F. Mexico
Phone: 55 5207 4347

#310
We Love Burgers
Cuisines: Burgers
Average price: Modest
Area: Condesa
Address: Michoacán 172
06140 México, D.F. Mexico
Phone: 55 6387 7704

#311
Pozolería Tixtla
Cuisines: Mexican
Average price: Modest
Area: Roma Norte
Address: Zacatecas 59
06700 México, D.F. Mexico
Phone: 55 5564 2859

#312
La Colomba de Veracroxe
Cuisines: Bistros
Average price: Expensive
Area: Condesa
Address: Veracruz 62
06700 México, D.F. Mexico
Phone: 55 5211 5835

#313
La Guapachosa
Cuisines: Mexican, Gastropubs
Average price: Modest
Area: Condesa
Address: Av. Oaxaca 31
06700 México, D.F. Mexico
Phone: 55 5531 7216

#314
El Exilio
Cuisines: Dive Bar, Mexican
Average price: Modest
Area: Centro Sur
Address: Peatonal San Jerónimo 38
06000 México, D.F. Mexico
Phone: 55 5709 0221

#315
Suntory
Cuisines: Japanese
Average price: Exclusive
Area: Del Valle
Address: Torres Adalid 14
03100 México, D.F. Mexico
Phone: 55 5536 9432

#316
El Rebost
Cuisines: Spanish
Average price: Modest
Area: Juárez
Address: Marsella 45
06600 México, D.F. Mexico
Phone: 55 5208 7171

#317
Restaurante Humbertos
Cuisines: Yucatan
Average price: Modest
Area: Del Valle
Address: Patricio Sanz 1440
03100 México, D.F. Mexico
Phone: 55 5559 8760

#318
Rojo Bistrot
Cuisines: French, Bistros
Average price: Exclusive
Area: Condesa
Address: Amsterdam 71
06140 México, D.F. Mexico
Phone: 55 5211 3705

#319
Garabatos
Cuisines: Mexican
Average price: Modest
Area: Polanco
Address: Presidente Masaryk 350
11560 México, D.F. Mexico
Phone: 55 5281 2603

#320
Vechio Fascino
Cuisines: Pizza
Average price: Modest
Area: Extremadura Insurgentes
Address: Millet 78
03740 México, D.F. Mexico
Phone: 55 5598 8120

#321
Taquería Los Chilangos
Cuisines: Tacos
Average price: Modest
Area: Centro Sur
Address: Motolinia 21
06000 México, D.F. Mexico
Phone: 55 5521 0470

#322
La Sonorita
Cuisines: Mexican, Barbeque
Average price: Expensive
Area: Cuauhtémoc
Address: Río Lerma 143
06500 México, D.F. Mexico
Phone: 55 5533 6702

#323
Burgers by Buba
Cuisines: Burgers
Average price: Modest
Area: Condesa
Address: Tamaulipas 72
06140 México, D.F. Mexico
Phone: 55 6286 0837

#324
Café Toscano
Cuisines: Cafeteria
Average price: Modest
Area: Polanco
Address: Tesmistocles 26
11550 México, D.F. Mexico
Phone: 55 6732 5374

#325
La Posta
Cuisines: Italian
Average price: Expensive
Area: Coyoacán
Address: Av. Pacífico 292
04020 México, D.F. Mexico
Phone: 55 5554 5538

#326
La Torre de Castilla
Cuisines: Spanish
Average price: Expensive
Area: Polanco
Address: Esopo 31
11550 México, D.F. Mexico
Phone: 55 5282 3540

#327
El Faraón Taquería
Cuisines: Tacos
Average price: Modest
Area: Condesa
Address: Oaxaca 92
06700 México, D.F. Mexico
Phone: 55 5514 2214

#328
Restaurante del Centro
Asturiano Polanco
Cuisines: Spanish
Average price: Expensive
Area: Polanco
Address: Calle Arquímedes 4
11550 México, D.F. Mexico
Phone: 55 5280 6362

#329
La Trainera
Cuisines: Seafood, Tacos
Average price: Expensive
Area: Polanco
Address: Alejandro Dumas 16
11550 México, D.F. Mexico
Phone: 55 5281 4338

#330
Pulquería Hermosa Hortensia
Cuisines: Dive Bar, Mexican
Average price: Inexpensive
Area: Centro Norte
Address: Callejón de la Amargura 4
06060 México, D.F. Mexico
Phone: 55 5529 7316

#331
Café Ruta de la Seda
Cuisines: Cafeteria
Average price: Modest
Area: Coyoacán
Address: Aurora 1 México, D.F. Mexico
Phone: 55 3869 2982

#332
Félix
Cuisines: Cocktail Bar
Average price: Modest
Area: Roma Norte
Address: Alvaro Obregón 64
06700 México, D.F. Mexico
Phone: 55 5264 0318

#333
Sirenito Blu
Cuisines: Seafood, Tacos
Average price: Modest
Area: Condesa
Address: Calle Pachuca 109
06140 México, D.F. Mexico
Phone: 55 5211 0267

#334
Matisse
Cuisines: Cafeteria
Average price: Modest
Area: Polanco
Address: Anatole France 115
11550 México, D.F. Mexico
Phone: 55 5281 8660

#335
Cluny
Cuisines: Creperies, French
Average price: Expensive
Area: San Ángel
Address: Avenida de la Paz 57
01000 México, D.F. Mexico
Phone: 55 5550 7359

#336
Fondue Haus
Cuisines: Fondue
Average price: Modest
Area: Nápoles
Address: Dakota 95
03810 México, D.F. Mexico
Phone: 55 6271 3330

#337
La Tía
Cuisines: Mexican, Diner
Average price: Inexpensive
Area: San Rafael
Address: Manuel María Contreras 20-A
06470 México, D.F. Mexico
Phone: 55 5546 0157

#338
La Bipo
Cuisines: Dive Bar
Average price: Modest
Area: Condesa
Address: Álvaro Obregón 287
06700 México, D.F. Mexico
Phone: 55 5525 4087

#339
Padam
Cuisines: French
Average price: Modest
Area: Condesa
Address: Veracruz 38 A
06700 México, D.F. Mexico
Phone: 55 5211 4931

#340
Mesón Puerto Chico
Cuisines: Spanish, Bar
Average price: Expensive
Area: Tabacalera
Address: José María Iglesias 55
06030 México, D.F. Mexico
Phone: 55 5705 6555

#341
Mibong
Cuisines: Vietnamese, Thai, Soup
Average price: Modest
Area: Condesa
Address: Campeche 396 B
06140 México, D.F. Mexico
Phone: 55 5211 2078

#342
El Samurai
Cuisines: Cefe
Average price: Expensive
Area: Nápoles
Address: Nueva York 85
03810 México, D.F. Mexico
Phone: 55 5523 1469

#343
Restaurante Hare Krishna
Cuisines: Vegetarian, Indian
Average price: Inexpensive
Area: San Miguel Chapultepec
Address: Tiburcio Montiel 45
11850 México, D.F. Mexico
Phone: 55 5272 5944

#344
Livorno
Cuisines: Italian
Average price: Modest
Area: Polanco
Address: Campos Elíseos No. 295
11550 México, D.F. Mexico
Phone: 55 5282 1001

#345
La Tiendita de San Pascual Bailongo
Cuisines: Pizza, Salad, Tapas/Small Plates
Average price: Modest
Area: Santa María la Ribera
Address: Sor Juana Inés de la Cruz 69
06400 México, D.F. Mexico
Phone: 55 5541 4215

#346
O´xacobeo
Cuisines: Spanish
Average price: Modest
Area: Roma Norte
Address: Colima 194, Col. Roma
06700 México, D.F. Mexico
Phone: 55 5511 8356

#347
Piloncillo y Cascabel
Cuisines: Diner
Average price: Inexpensive
Area: Del Valle
Address: Torres Adalid 1263
03020 México, D.F. Mexico
Phone: 55 3330 2121

#348
Fritz
Cuisines: German, Bar
Average price: Expensive
Area: Doctores
Address: Doctor Río de la Loza 221
06720 México, D.F. Mexico
Phone: 55 3096 8696

#349
Matisse
Cuisines: Mexican, Bar,
Patisserie/Cake Shop
Average price: Modest
Area: Condesa
Address: Av. Amsterdam 260
06100 México, D.F. Mexico
Phone: 55 5584 3210

#350
Cafebrería El Péndulo
Cuisines: BookStore, Cafeteria
Average price: Modest
Area: Condesa
Address: Nuevo León 115
06100 México, D.F. Mexico
Phone: 55 5286 9493

#351
La EnoTK
Cuisines: Italian, Wine Bar
Average price: Expensive
Area: Polanco
Address: Presidente Masaryk 298
11560 México, D.F. Mexico
Phone: 55 5281 8212

#352
La Barraca Valenciana
Cuisines: Spanish, Delis
Average price: Modest
Area: Coyoacán
Address: Centenario 91-C
04100 México, D.F. Mexico
Phone: 55 5658 1880

#353
Conde Sandwich Bar
Cuisines: Sandwiches
Average price: Modest
Area: Roma Norte
Address: Cordoba 84
06700 México, D.F. Mexico
Phone: 55 4427 4683

#354
Antojitos Yucatecos Los Arcos
Cuisines: Yucatan
Average price: Modest
Area: Juárez
Address: Florencia 43
06600 México, D.F. Mexico
Phone: 55 5533 5877

#355
La Casa del Pastor, Polanco
Cuisines: Mexican
Average price: Modest
Area: Polanco
Address: Av. Alfredo de Musset 3
11560 México, D.F. Mexico
Phone: 55 5281 8813

#356
Tacos de Canasta Chucho
Cuisines: Mexican
Average price: Inexpensive
Area: Centro Sur
Address: Av. 5 de Mayo 17
06010 México, D.F. Mexico
Phone: 55 5521 0280

#357
Pata Negra Cuauhtémoc
Cuisines: Tapas/Small Plates
Average price: Modest
Area: Cuauhtémoc
Address: Río Niágara 43, Col. Cuahtémoc
06500 México, D.F. Mexico
Phone: 55 5525 9712

#358
Dulcinea
Cuisines: Seafood, Mexican
Average price: Expensive
Area: Roma Norte
Address: Tabasco 46
06700 México, D.F. Mexico
Phone: 55 9688 6595

#359
Macondo
Cuisines: Colombian
Average price: Modest
Area: Roma Sur
Address: Medellín 224
06700 México, D.F. Mexico
Phone: 55 5264 1362

#360
La Casa de Toño
Cuisines: Mexican
Average price: Inexpensive
Area: Nápoles
Address: Montecito 38
03810 México, D.F. Mexico
Phone: 55 5386 1125

#361
La Pizzería Argentina
Cuisines: Pizza
Average price: Modest
Area: Roma Sur
Address: Tlacotalpan 116
06760 México, D.F. Mexico
Phone: 55 5264 5271

#362
La casa de la Yeya Condesa
Cuisines: Mexican
Average price: Modest
Area: Condesa
Address: Citlaltepetl 25, Col.Condesa
06170 México, D.F. Mexico
Phone: 55 5211 4514

#363
Burger OK
Cuisines: Burgers
Average price: Modest
Area: Cuauhtémoc
Address: Río Amazonas 23A
06500 México, D.F. Mexico
Phone: 55 5603 6355

#364
Mesa Nápoles
Cuisines: Mexican, Fast Food
Average price: Modest
Area: Nápoles
Address: Kansas 38
03840 México, D.F. Mexico
Phone: 55 5669 2373

#365
Frutos Prohibidos y Otros Placeres
Cuisines: Salad, Sandwiches
Average price: Modest
Area: Del Valle
Address: Pestalozzi 1166, local D
03100 México, D.F. Mexico
Phone: 55 5601 4340

#366
Restaurante Bar Chon
Cuisines: Mexican
Average price: Expensive
Area: Centro Sur
Address: Regina 160
06090 México, D.F. Mexico
Phone: 55 5542 0873

#367
Tori Tori Temistocles
Cuisines: Japanese
Average price: Expensive
Area: Polanco
Address: Temistocles 61
11550 México, D.F. Mexico
Phone: 55 5281 8112

#368
Monsieur Croque
Cuisines: French
Average price: Modest
Area: Condesa
Address: Av. Tamaulipas 39
06140 México, D.F. Mexico
Phone: 55 5211 7898

#369
Musuko
Cuisines: Japanese
Average price: Modest
Area: Condesa
Address: Nuevo León 160
06170 México, D.F. Mexico
Phone: 55 5553 1443

#370
Churros Jordan
Cuisines: Cafeteria
Average price: Inexpensive
Area: Coyoacán
Address: Aguayo 7
04100 México, D.F. Mexico
Phone: 55 7090 8706

#371
Lactography
Cuisines: Cheese Shop, Grocery, Sandwiches, Cheese Tasting Classes
Average price: Modest
Area: Roma Norte
Address: Querétaro 225
06700 México, D.F. Mexico
Phone: 55 5264 8270

#372
Barrio Sur
Cuisines: Argentine, Italian
Average price: Modest
Area: San Ángel
Address: Calzada Santa Catarina 207, San Angel Inn, Álvaro Obregón
01060 México, D.F. Mexico
Phone: 55 5550 4716

#373
Brew & Botana
Cuisines: Beer Bar, Mexican
Average price: Modest
Area: Tabacalera
Address: Calle Thomas Alva Edison 35
06030 México, D.F. Mexico
Phone: 55 5535 0601

#374
La Ruota
Cuisines: Cafeteria, Italian
Average price: Modest
Area: Condesa
Address: Av. México 121
04100 México, D.F. Mexico
Phone: 55 5574 7464

#375
Asia Perú
Cuisines: Peruvian
Average price: Modest
Area: Condesa
Address: Benjamín Franklin 239
06140 México, D.F. Mexico
Phone: 55 6363 6891

#376
Central de Pizzas
Cuisines: Pizza, Argentine
Average price: Modest
Area: Escandón
Address: Astrónomos 20
11800 México, D.F. Mexico
Phone: 55 6236 7933

#377
Balboa Pizzeria
Cuisines: Pizza, Italian
Average price: Modest
Area: Cuauhtémoc
Address: Río Lerma 94
06500 México, D.F. Mexico
Phone: 55 5207 3476

#378
Mikasa
Cuisines: Ethnic Food, Sushi Bar
Average price: Modest
Area: Roma Norte
Address: San Luis Potosí 173
06700 México, D.F. Mexico
Phone: 55 5584 3430

#379
Cantina La Única de Guerrero
Cuisines: Dive Bar, Mexican
Average price: Modest
Area: Buenavista
Address: Guerrero 258
06300 México, D.F. Mexico
Phone: 55 5526 8394

#380
Blossom
Cuisines: Chinese
Average price: Expensive
Area: Del Valle
Address: San Francisco 360
03100 México, D.F. Mexico
Phone: 55 5523 8516

#381
Hansa
Cuisines: Organic Store, Vegetarian
Average price: Expensive
Area: Polanco
Address: Euler 145-149
11550 México, D.F. Mexico
Phone: 55 5531 4566

#382
La rambla
Cuisines: Pizza, Barbeque
Average price: Modest
Area: Condesa
Address: Ometusco entre Benjamin Hill
y Baja California. 06140 México, D.F. Mexico
Phone: 55 5515 1374

#383
Gloutonnerie
Cuisines: French
Average price: Exclusive
Area: Polanco
Address: Campos Elíseos 142
11550 México, D.F. Mexico
Phone: 55 5250 3550

#384
Barbacoa de Santiago
Cuisines: Mexican
Average price: Modest
Area: Nápoles
Address: Av. San Antonio 57
03810 México, D.F. Mexico
Phone: 55 5543 5047

#385
Bistro 83
Cuisines: French, Mexican
Average price: Expensive
Area: San Ángel
Address: Amargura 17
01000 México, D.F. Mexico
Phone: 55 5616 4911

#386
Valentina
Cuisines: Cafeteria
Average price: Inexpensive
Area: Cuauhtémoc
Address: Guadalquivir 31
06500 México, D.F. Mexico
Phone: 55 5207 2905

#387
Ramen-Ya
Cuisines: Ramen
Average price: Modest
Area: Del Valle
Address: Fresas 59
03100 México, D.F. Mexico
Phone: 55 5559 1495

#388
El Villamelón
Cuisines: Tacos
Average price: Inexpensive
Area: Ciudad de los Deportes
Address: Tintoreto 123
03710 México, D.F. Mexico
Phone: 55 1042 2352

#389
Carlotta
Cuisines: Mexican
Average price: Expensive
Area: Polanco
Address: Campos Elíseos 290
11560 México, D.F. Mexico
Phone: 55 5281 0292

#390
Alexis Gyros
Cuisines: Mediterranean, Greek
Average price: Modest
Area: Roma Sur
Address: Manzanillo 122
06760 México, D.F. Mexico
Phone: 55 7572 2069

#391
Adonis
Cuisines: Arabian
Average price: Expensive
Area: Polanco
Address: Homero 424
11550 México, D.F. Mexico
Phone: 55 5531 8081

#392
La Habana
Cuisines: Cuban, Cafeteria
Average price: Modest
Area: Juárez
Address: Morelos 62
06600 México, D.F. Mexico
Phone: 55 5546 0255

#393
Mingo's Condesa
Cuisines: Delis, Food
Average price: Inexpensive
Area: Condesa
Address: Zamora 31
06140 México, D.F. Mexico
Phone: 55 4623 7962

#394
El Asado Argentino
Cuisines: Argentine
Average price: Expensive
Area: Juárez
Address: Dinamarca 72
06600 México, D.F. Mexico
Phone: 55 5592 7071

#395
Séptimo
Cuisines: Pizza, Italian
Average price: Expensive
Area: Coyoacán
Address: Venustiano Carranza 106
04000 México, D.F. Mexico
Phone: 55 5658 0571

#396
Paprika
Cuisines: Moroccan, Arabian
Average price: Modest
Area: Juárez
Address: Calle Marsella 61
01810 México, D.F. Mexico
Phone: 55 5533 0303

#397
I. Carbón
Cuisines: Burgers
Average price: Inexpensive
Area: Roma Norte
Address: Tonala S/N
06500 México, D.F. Mexico
Phone: 55 5207 8568

#398
Bukowski's Bar
Cuisines: Jazz & Blues
Average price: Modest
Area: Juárez
Address: Hamburgo 126
06600 México, D.F. Mexico
Phone: 55 5208 2327

#399
Bó Pastisseria
Cuisines: Bakeries, Patisserie/Cake Shop
Average price: Expensive
Area: Condesa
Address: Av. Sonora 174
06140 México, D.F. Mexico
Phone: 55 4622 7050

#400
Los Portales de Tlaquepaque
Cuisines: Dive Bar
Average price: Inexpensive
Area: Obrera
Address: Bolívar 56
06800 México, D.F. Mexico
Phone: 55 5518 6344

#401
Tierra Garat
Cuisines: Coffee & Tea, Breakfast & Brunch
Average price: Inexpensive
Area: Roma Norte
Address: Local 4
06700 México, D.F. Mexico
Phone: 55 5207 6298

#402
Don Deme
Cuisines: Diner
Average price: Inexpensive
Area: Roma Norte
Address: Tonalá s/n
06700 México, D.F. Mexico
Phone: 55 5264 8912

#403
Nonsolo Express Cuauhtémoc
Cuisines: Italian, Mediterranean
Average price: Modest
Area: Cuauhtémoc
Address: Rio Lerma 187
06500 México, D.F. Mexico
Phone: 55 5511 2074

#404
Rokai-Ramen
Cuisines: Ramen
Average price: Expensive
Area: Cuauhtémoc
Address: Río Ebro 89
06500 México, D.F. Mexico
Phone: 55 5207 7543

#405
Warung Makan Comida Indonesia
Cuisines: Asian Fusion
Average price: Modest
Area: Condesa
Address: Puebla 341
06700 México, D.F. Mexico
Phone: 55 6548 2708

#406
Comfort Food
Cuisines: Cafeteria, Breakfast & Brunch
Average price: Inexpensive
Area: Narvarte
Address: Cumbres de Maltrata 390 - E
03020 México, D.F. Mexico
Phone: 55 6823 3331

#407
La Strega
Cuisines: Cefe
Average price: Expensive
Area: Nápoles
Address: Maricopa 11
03810 México, D.F. Mexico
Phone: 55 5669 4080

#408
Restaurante Azul y Oro
Cuisines: Mexican
Average price: Expensive
Area: Ciudad Universitaria
Address: Insurgentes Sur 3000
53160 México, D.F. Mexico
Phone: 55 5622 7135

#409
La Guanajuatense
Cuisines: Mexican
Average price: Modest
Area: Cuauhtémoc
Address: Rio Lerma 262
06500 México, D.F. Mexico
Phone: 55 5208 7931

#410
Creperie de la Paix
Cuisines: Creperies, French
Average price: Modest
Area: Condesa
Address: Av. Michoacán 103
06140 México, D.F. Mexico
Phone: 55 5286 0049

#411
Falafelito
Cuisines: Vegan, Vegetarian
Average price: Inexpensive
Area: Condesa
Address: Av. México 105
06100 México, D.F. Mexico
Phone: 55 5264 8024

#412
Salón Covadonga
Cuisines: Dive Bar, Spanish
Average price: Modest
Area: Roma Norte
Address: Puebla 121
06700 México, D.F. Mexico
Phone: 55 5533 2922

#413
Merendero Las Lupitas
Cuisines: Mexican
Average price: Modest
Area: Coyoacán
Address: Plaza Santa Catarina 4
01060 México, D.F. Mexico
Phone: 55 5554 3353

#414
La Romita
Cuisines: Beer Bar, Cocktail Bar, Seafood
Average price: Modest
Area: Roma Sur
Address: Coahuila 185
06700 México, D.F. Mexico
Phone: 55 6361 4385

#415
Lonchería María Isabel
Cuisines: Mexican
Average price: Modest
Area: Polanco
Address: Emilio Castelar 14
11560 México, D.F. Mexico
Phone: 55 5281 3835

#416
Círculo del Sureste
Cuisines: Bar, Yucatan
Average price: Expensive
Area: Juárez
Address: Calle Lucerna 12
06600 México, D.F. Mexico
Phone: 55 5535 2704

#417
Reforma 500
Cuisines: Latin American
Average price: Expensive
Area: Juárez
Address: Paseo de la Reforma 500
06600 México, D.F. Mexico
Phone: 55 5230 1818

#418
La Ciudad de Colima
Cuisines: Salad, Sandwiches
Average price: Inexpensive
Area: Polanco
Address: Av. Horacio 522 Local C
11570 México, D.F. Mexico
Phone: 55 5545 2719

#419
Sartenazo Fast
Cuisines: Vietnamese, Middle Eastern
Average price: Modest
Area: Tabacalera
Address: Ezequiel Montes 23
06030 México, D.F. Mexico
Phone: 55 4615 0121

#420
Zoku Por Hiroshi
Cuisines: Japanese, Sushi Bar
Average price: Expensive
Area: Condesa
Address: Calle Durango 359
06700 México, D.F. Mexico
Phone: 55 5211 9855

#421
El Chilaquilito
Cuisines: Mexican
Average price: Modest
Area: Postal
Address: Correspondencia 176
03410 México, D.F. Mexico
Phone: 55 1579 8981

#422
Ruben's
Cuisines: Burgers
Average price: Modest
Area: Polanco
Address: Isaac Newton 93
11550 México, D.F. Mexico
Phone: 55 5203 2994

#423
Mesón Antigua Sta Catarina
Cuisines: Mexican
Average price: Expensive
Area: Coyoacán
Address: Jardín Santa Catarina 6
04010 México, D.F. Mexico
Phone: 55 5659 3003

#424
Sonora Grill Prime
Cuisines: Steakhouse, Mexican
Average price: Exclusive
Area: Polanco
Address: Presidente Masaryk 360
11550 México, D.F. Mexico
Phone: 55 5280 7328

#425
Centro Cultural de Yoga Prabhupada
Cuisines: Social Club, Indian, Guest House
Average price: Inexpensive
Area: Centro Norte
Address: Allende 33
06000 México, D.F. Mexico
Phone: 55 5529 5375

#426
Restaurante Casa
Club del Académico
Cuisines: Italian
Average price: Expensive
Area: Pedregal
Address: Av. Ciudad Universitaria 301
04510 México, D.F. Mexico
Phone: 55 5616 1558

#427
Tokyo Rose
Cuisines: Japanese
Average price: Modest
Area: Narvarte
Address: Xola 1604
03020 México, D.F. Mexico
Phone: 55 5530 8021

#428
Viko
Cuisines: Street Vendor, Tacos
Average price: Inexpensive
Area: Cuauhtémoc
Address: Paseo de la Reforma S/N
06600 México, D.F. Mexico
Phone: 55 2747 8475

#429
Café El Jarocho
Cuisines: Cafeteria
Average price: Inexpensive
Area: Coyoacán
Address: Cuauhtémoc 134
04100 México, D.F. Mexico
Phone: 55 5418 5658

#430
Tacos Los Bigotes
Cuisines: Mexican
Average price: Inexpensive
Area: Del Valle
Address: Amores 1553
03100 México, D.F. Mexico
Phone: 55 5335 1587

#431
Litoral
Cuisines: Seafood, Japanese
Average price: Expensive
Area: Condesa
Address: Tamaulipas 55
06140 México, D.F. Mexico
Phone: 55 5286 2025

#432
Bar Mancera
Cuisines: Spanish
Average price: Expensive
Area: Centro Sur
Address: Venustiano Carranza 49
06010 México, D.F. Mexico
Phone: 55 5521 9755

#433
Asian Bay
Cuisines: Chinese
Average price: Modest
Area: Condesa
Address: Tamaulipas 95
06170 México, D.F. Mexico
Phone: 55 5553 4582

#434
Los Tres Coyotes
Cuisines: Tacos
Average price: Modest
Area: Coyoacán
Address: Miguel Ángel de Quevedo 654
04010 México, D.F. Mexico
Phone: 55 5554 6798

#435
Arre Sonora
Cuisines: Tacos, Northern Mexican
Average price: Modest
Area: Álamos
Address: Isabel la Católica 546-B
03400 México, D.F. Mexico
Phone: 55 6796 4301

#436
Lázaro Comedor & Bar
Cuisines: Mexican, Cocktail Bar
Average price: Expensive
Area: Roma Norte
Address: Frontera 150
06700 México, D.F. Mexico
Phone: 55 6725 4032

#437
Ermitaño
Cuisines: Pizza
Average price: Inexpensive
Area: Coyoacán
Address: Av. Miguel Ángel de Quevedo 754
04010 México, D.F. Mexico
Phone: 55 4437 7111

#438
Boicotcafe
Cuisines: Cafeteria
Average price: Modest
Area: Roma Norte
Address: Jalapa 99
06700 México, D.F. Mexico
Phone: 55 6845 6037

#439
La Casa de los Abuelos
Cuisines: Cefe, Bakeries
Average price: Modest
Area: Polanco
Address: Moliere 325
11550 México, D.F. Mexico
Phone: 55 5203 0159

#440
Specia
Cuisines: Cefe
Average price: Expensive
Area: Condesa
Address: Amsterdam 241
06140 México, D.F. Mexico
Phone: 55 5564 1367

#441
La Lorena
Cuisines: Bakeries, British
Average price: Expensive
Area: Las Lomas
Address: Monte Líbano 265
11000 México, D.F. Mexico
Phone: 55 5202 4594

#442
La Madrileña
Cuisines: Diner, Delis
Average price: Inexpensive
Area: Del Valle
Address: Pilares 416
03100 México, D.F. Mexico
Phone: 55 5605 5757

#443
Dondonburi
Cuisines: Sushi Bar, Japanese
Average price: Inexpensive
Area: Del Valle
Address: Miguel Laurent 112-113
03200 México, D.F. Mexico
Phone: 55 6796 1213

#444
Jetson's
Cuisines: Bar
Average price: Modest
Area: Condesa
Address: Av. Álvaro Obregón 291
06100 México, D.F. Mexico
Phone: 55 5533 5985

#445
The Ramen House
Cuisines: Korean, Ramen
Average price: Inexpensive
Area: Cuauhtémoc
Address: Río Pánuco 132
06500 México, D.F. Mexico
Phone: 55 6545 9513

#446
Roldán 37
Cuisines: Mexican
Average price: Expensive
Area: Centro Sur
Address: Calle Roldán 37
06000 México, D.F. Mexico
Phone: 55 5542 1951

#447
La Loggia
Cuisines: Italian
Average price: Expensive
Area: Polanco
Address: Emilio Castelar 44
11510 México, D.F. Mexico
Phone: 55 5280 4807

#448
El Venadito
Cuisines: Tacos
Average price: Inexpensive
Area: Florida
Address: Universidad 1701
01050 México, D.F. Mexico
Phone: 55 5661 9786

#449
Cancino
Cuisines: Pizza, Italian, Beer Bar
Average price: Modest
Area: San Miguel Chapultepec
Address: Gobernador Rafael Rebollar 95
11850 México, D.F. Mexico
Phone: 55 4333 0770

#450
Sliders Burger Shop
Cuisines: Burgers, Hot Dogs, Sandwiches
Average price: Modest
Area: Polanco
Address: Virgilio 25
04489 México, D.F. Mexico
Phone: 55 5281 5380

#451
Roma Quince
Cuisines: Fashion, Mexican, Home Decor
Average price: Expensive
Area: Condesa
Address: Medellin 67
06700 México, D.F. Mexico
Phone: 55 5207 8682

#452
El Japonez
Cuisines: Japanese
Average price: Expensive
Area: Polanco
Address: Emilio Castelar 135
11550 México, D.F. Mexico
Phone: 55 4434 4053

#453
Cambalache
Cuisines: Argentine
Average price: Expensive
Area: Del Valle
Address: Insurgentes Sur 1384
03100 México, D.F. Mexico
Phone: 55 5534 5858

#454
La Cicciolina y sus pecados
Cuisines: Modern European
Average price: Modest
Area: Cuauhtémoc
Address: Río Nilo #90, Esquina
con Reforma. Colonia Cuauhtémoc
06500 México, D.F. Mexico
Phone: 55 5514 9533

#455
Lonchería La Rambla
Cuisines: Cefe
Average price: Inexpensive
Area: Centro Sur
Address: Motolinia 38
06020 México, D.F. Mexico
Phone: 99 137 42958

#456
Mi Gusto Es
Cuisines: Seafood, Fish & Chips, Mexican
Average price: Modest
Area: Polanco
Address: Torcuato Tasso 324
11560 México, D.F. Mexico
Phone: 55 5254 5678

#457
Los Sopes de la Nueve
Cuisines: Mexican
Average price: Inexpensive
Area: San Simón Ticumán
Address: Luis Spota 85
03660 México, D.F. Mexico
Phone: 52 553 23502

#458
Café Los Baristas
Cuisines: Cafeteria
Average price: Inexpensive
Area: Ciudad Universitaria
Address: Cto. Escolar 62
04360 México, D.F. Mexico
Phone: 55 2535 5156

#459
Cobá Fonda Yucateca
Cuisines: Yucatan
Average price: Inexpensive
Area: Del Valle
Address: Av. Universidad 635
03100 México, D.F. Mexico
Phone: 55 6395 9961

#460
Cabo Polonio
Cuisines: Pizza, Food
Average price: Modest
Area: Condesa
Address: Zamora 48
06140 México, D.F. Mexico
Phone: 55 5609 0145

#461
Gran Buffet - Bar La Isla del Dragón
Cuisines: Cefe
Average price: Inexpensive
Area: Centro Sur
Address: Filomeno Mata 15, Col. Centro,
Deleg. Cuauhtémoc
06010 México, D.F. Mexico
Phone: 55 5518 0202

#462
Dada X
Cuisines:
Average price: Modest
Area: Roma Norte, Doctores
Address: Av. Cuauhtémoc 39
09819 México, D.F. Mexico
Phone: 55 6279 8717

#463
Cantina La No. 20
Cuisines: Mexican, Dive Bar
Average price: Expensive
Area: Polanco
Address: Andrés Bello 10
11550 México, D.F. Mexico
Phone: 55 5281 3524

#464
El Ocho
Cuisines: Cafeteria, Breakfast & Brunch
Average price: Modest
Area: Roma Norte
Address: Plaza Luis Cabrera 16
06700 México, D.F. Mexico
Phone: 55 5264 5070

#465
La Locanda
Cuisines: Italian
Average price: Expensive
Area: San Ángel
Address: Av. de La Paz 23
01000 México, D.F. Mexico
Phone: 55 5550 4260

#466
Nobu Polanco
Cuisines: Asian Fusion
Average price: Exclusive
Area: Polanco
Address: Anatole France 74
11550 México, D.F. Mexico
Phone: 55 5280 2945

#467
Texas de Brazil
Cuisines: Brazilian, Steakhouse
Average price: Expensive
Area: Polanco
Address: Newton 62
11550 México, D.F. Mexico
Phone: 55 5280 1688

#468
Café Ó
Cuisines: Cafeteria
Average price: Expensive
Area: Las Lomas
Address: Monte Líbano 245
11000 México, D.F. Mexico
Phone: 55 5520 9227

#469
Tlacoyotitlán
Cuisines: Mexican
Average price: Modest
Area: Santa María la Ribera
Address: Díaz Miron 84
06400 México, D.F. Mexico
Phone: 55 6588 7459

#470
Bistro Michellena
Cuisines: Cafeteria, Bistros, Burgers
Average price: Modest
Area: Cuauhtémoc
Address: Rio Tigris 22
06500 México, D.F. Mexico
Phone: 55 5511 2613

#471
La destilería
Cuisines: Mexican
Average price: Modest
Area: Juárez
Address: Reforma 222, Juárez
06600 México, D.F. Mexico
Phone: 55 5514 2393

#472
Crisanta Garage
Cuisines: Bar, Mexican
Average price: Modest
Area: Tabacalera
Address: Plaza de la República 51
06030 México, D.F. Mexico
Phone: 55 5535 6372

#473
Tori Tori
Cuisines: Sushi Bar, Japanese
Average price: Expensive
Area: Condesa
Address: Av. Amsterdam 219
06140 México, D.F. Mexico
Phone: 55 5264 3466

#474
El Regreso
Cuisines: Mexican
Average price: Inexpensive
Area: Del Valle
Address: Obrero Mundial 383 B
03020 México, D.F. Mexico
Phone: 55 5639 3377

#475
Tortería Royalty
Cuisines: Delis
Average price: Inexpensive
Area: Polanco
Address: Horacio 227, Col. Polanco
11550 México, D.F. Mexico
Phone: 55 5250 2118

#476
San Nicolas DF
Cuisines: Mediterranean, Specialty Food
Average price: Modest
Area: Roma Sur
Address: Av. Baja California 39
06760 México, D.F. Mexico
Phone: 55 5467 6052

#477
Mama Rumba
Cuisines: Dance Club, Cuban
Average price: Expensive
Area: Roma Norte
Address: Querétaro 230
06700 México, D.F. Mexico
Phone: 55 5564 6920

#478
Min Sok Chon
Cuisines: Korean
Average price: Modest
Area: Juárez
Address: Florencia 45
06600 México, D.F. Mexico
Phone: 55 5207 8506

#479
Don Pollo
Cuisines: Mexican
Average price: Modest
Area: Juárez
Address: Paseo de la Reforma 264
06500 México, D.F. Mexico
Phone: 99 164 14835

#480
Jack House Tennessee
Cuisines: American, Barbeque, Beer Bar
Average price: Modest
Area: Condesa
Address: Tamaulipas 80
06140 México, D.F. Mexico
Phone: 55 5211 8397

#481
Tacos Gus
Cuisines: Mexican
Average price: Inexpensive
Area: Polanco
Address: Séneca 446
11550 México, D.F. Mexico
Phone: 55 6268 6390

#482
Churrerías del Convento
Cuisines: Mexican, Churros
Average price: Inexpensive
Area: San Ángel
Address: Av. de la Paz 58-B
01000 México, D.F. Mexico
Phone: 55 5913 4670

#483
Hacienda de Cortés
Cuisines: Cefe
Average price: Modest
Area: Coyoacán
Address: Fernández Leal 70
04000 México, D.F. Mexico
Phone: 55 5659 3741

#484
La Chula
Cuisines: Tacos
Average price: Modest
Area: Escandón
Address: Astrónomos 61
11800 México, D.F. Mexico
Phone: 55 5523 4040

#485
Confit
Cuisines: Mexican, French
Average price: Expensive
Area: Polanco
Address: Séneca 49
11550 México, D.F. Mexico
Phone: 55 4336 0450

#486
Decrab
Cuisines: Mexican
Average price: Expensive
Area: Las Lomas
Address: Prado Rte 395
11000 México, D.F. Mexico
Phone: 55 2623 2703

#487
Fonda Argentina
Cuisines: Argentine, Steakhouse
Average price: Expensive
Area: Independencia
Address: Isabel la Católica 1198
03630 México, D.F. Mexico
Phone: 55 5539 1617

#488
Dulce Olivia
Cuisines: Cafeteria, Art Galleries
Average price: Modest
Area: Coyoacán
Address: Pino 79
04010 México, D.F. Mexico
Phone: 55 5672 8748

#489
Campotoro
Cuisines: Seafood, Mediterranean
Average price: Expensive
Area: Polanco
Address: Anatole France 70
11560 México, D.F. Mexico
Phone: 55 5281 7093

#490
Lynis
Cuisines: Cafeteria
Average price: Inexpensive
Area: Escandón
Address: Av. Nuevo León 255
06100 México, D.F. Mexico
Phone: 55 6363 6961

#491
La Parrilla Quilmes
Cuisines: Argentine
Average price: Expensive
Area: Condesa
Address: Alfonso Reyes 193
06100 México, D.F. Mexico
Phone: 55 5276 2652

#492
Gruta Ehden
Cuisines: Arabian
Average price: Expensive
Area: Florida
Address: Pino 69
01030 México, D.F. Mexico
Phone: 55 5661 1994

#493
Mi Gusto Es
Cuisines: Seafood, Fish & Chips, Mexican
Average price: Expensive
Area: Narvarte
Address: Diagonal San Antonio 1709 C
03600 México, D.F. Mexico
Phone: 55 5235 3217

#494
Salón Corona
Cuisines: Bar, Mexican
Average price: Modest
Area: Centro Sur
Address: Bolívar 24
06000 México, D.F. Mexico
Phone: 55 5512 5725

#495
La Parroquia de Veracruz
Cuisines: Cafeteria, Mexican
Average price: Modest
Area: Florida
Address: Insurgentes Sur 1870
03200 México, D.F. Mexico
Phone: 229 217 3708

#496
Delisa
Cuisines: Cafeteria, Bakeries, Sandwiches
Average price: Modest
Area: Roma Norte
Address: Tabasco 139
06700 México, D.F. Mexico
Phone: 55 5511 5745

#497
Potzolcano
Cuisines: Mexican
Average price: Inexpensive
Area: América
Address: Av. Observatorio 409
01120 México, D.F. Mexico
Phone: 55 2614 6396

#498
Restaurante Las Costillas
Cuisines: Barbeque, Tacos
Average price: Modest
Area: Condesa
Address: Juan Escutia 104
06140 México, D.F. Mexico
Phone: 55 5286 2700

#499
El Grill Oh!
Cuisines: Burgers
Average price: Modest
Area: San Pedro de Los Pinos
Address: Avenida 3 82
03800 México, D.F. Mexico
Phone: 55 6365 3003

#500
Caldos de Pollo Polanco
Cuisines: Cefe, Food
Average price: Inexpensive
Area: Polanco
Address: Ejercito Nacional 838
11540 México, D.F. Mexico
Phone: 55 5280 5850

16466801R00029

Made in the USA
Middletown, DE
23 November 2018